Alan Titchmarsh
how to garden

Growing
Roses

Alan **Titchmarsh**
how to garden

Growing Roses

BOOKS

10 9 8 7 6 5 4 3 2 1

Published in 2011 by BBC Books, an imprint of
Ebury Publishing, a Random House Group Company

The Random House Group Limited Reg. No. 954009

Addresses for companies within the Random House
Group can be found at www.randomhouse.co.uk

The Random House Group Limited
supports The Forest Stewardship
Council (FSC), the leading
international forest certification
organisation. All our titles that are
printed on Greenpeace approved
FSC certified paper carry the FSC
logo. Our paper procurement
policy can be found at www.
rbooks.co.uk/environment

FSC
www.fsc.org
MIX
Paper from
responsible sources
FSC™ C004592

A CIP catalogue record for this book is available from
the British Library.

ISBN 978 1 84 607408 0

Produced by OutHouse!
Shalbourne, Marlborough, Wiltshire SN8 3QJ

BBC BOOKS
COMMISSIONING EDITOR: Lorna Russell
PROJECT EDITOR: Caroline McArthur
PRODUCTION: Rebecca Jones

OUTHOUSE!
COMMISSIONING EDITOR: Sue Gordon
SERIES EDITOR & PROJECT EDITOR: Polly Boyd
SERIES ART DIRECTOR: Robin Whitecross
CONTRIBUTING EDITOR: Andrew McIndoe
DESIGNERS: Heather McCarry, Louise Turpin
ILLUSTRATIONS by Lizzie Harper, Susan Hillier,
Janet Tanner
PHOTOGRAPHS by Jonathan Buckley except where
credited otherwise on page 128
CONCEPT DEVELOPMENT & SERIES DESIGN:
Elizabeth Mallard-Shaw, Sharon Cluett

Colour origination by Altaimage, London
Printed and bound by Firmengruppe APPL,
Wemding, Germany

Contents

Introduction

Gardening is one of the best and most fulfilling activities on earth, but it can sometimes seem complicated and confusing. The answers to problems can usually be found in books, but big fat gardening books can be rather daunting. Where do you start? How can you find just the information you want without wading through lots of stuff that is not appropriate to your particular problem? Well, a good index is helpful, but sometimes a smaller book devoted to one particular subject fits the bill better – especially if it is reasonably priced and if you have a small garden where you might not be able to fit in everything suggested in a larger volume.

The *How to Garden* books aim to fill that gap – even if sometimes it may be only a small one. They are clearly set out and written, I hope, in a straightforward, easy-to-understand style. I don't see any point in making gardening complicated, when much of it is based on common sense and observation. (All the key techniques are explained and illustrated, and I've included plenty of tips and tricks of the trade.)

There are suggestions on the best plants and the best varieties to grow in particular situations and for a particular effect. I've tried to keep the information crisp and to the point so that you can find what you need quickly and easily and then put your new-found knowledge into practice. Don't worry if you're not familiar with the Latin names of plants. They are there to make sure you can find the plant as it will be labelled in the nursery or garden centre, but where appropriate I have included common names, too. Forgetting a plant's name need not stand in your way when it comes to being able to grow it.

Above all, the *How to Garden* books are designed to fill you with passion and enthusiasm for your garden and all that its creation and care entails, from designing and planting it to maintaining it and enjoying it. For more than fifty years gardening has been my passion, and that initial enthusiasm for watching plants grow, for trying something new and for just being outside pottering has never faded. If anything I am keener on gardening now than I ever was and get more satisfaction from my plants every day. It's not that I am simply a romantic, but rather that I have learned to look for the good in gardens and in plants, and there is lots to be found. Oh, there are times when I fail – when my plants don't grow as well as they should and I need to try harder. But where would I rather be on a sunny day? Nowhere!

The *How to Garden* handbooks will, I hope, allow some of that enthusiasm – childish though it may be – to rub off on you, and the information they contain will, I hope, make you a better gardener, as well as opening your eyes to the magic of plants and flowers.

Introducing roses

Roses are the most exquisite and cherished of all flowers. Although sometimes challenging to grow, they're among the most rewarding of garden plants, captivating us with their soft, sensual petals, ravishing colours and beguiling perfume. Gardeners have enjoyed a long-lasting love affair with the rose, and despite brief infatuations with other blooms our passion for roses is as strong today as it has ever been. Perhaps the interest is kept alive by the creation of new varieties – the ongoing quest of the plant breeder to improve on perfection. Or perhaps it is because roses are such versatile shrubs that can be used in our gardens in so many different ways.

Roses in gardens past and present

It is generally believed that roses were first cultivated about 5,000 years ago. It probably all started in China, but the ancient Egyptians were also great rose growers, as were the Greeks and the Arabians. The Romans established public rose gardens and grew roses for their petals, which were used as a source of perfume, for confetti in ceremonies and celebrations, and for medicinal purposes.

The lovely old blush China rose (*Rosa × odorata* 'Pallida') was the first repeat-flowering rose to be introduced to Europe from China.

The apothecary's rose (*Rosa gallica* var. *officinalis*) has been growing in European gardens for over 900 years.

After the fall of the Roman empire the popularity of the rose declined and it found refuge in the gardens of monks and medics, coming to the fore again when knights brought back new species on their return from the Crusades. It may be that *Rosa gallica* made its way from France to England via a crusader in the 12th century. *Rosa gallica* var. *officinalis*, known as the apothecary's rose because of its value in early medicine, is still a good rose for today's gardens. Incidentally, *officinalis* means 'of the shop', referring to the apothecary's shop. The striped form, *Rosa gallica* 'Versicolor', is also still popular;

formerly known as *Rosa mundi*, it was named after 'Fair Rosamund', the mistress of Henry II.

In the 15th century the rose made its debut in politics. It was adopted as the symbol for the Houses of York and Lancaster, both of which were vying for control of England. The white rose symbolized York and the red rose Lancaster – hence the Wars of the Roses. Although the hostilities have long ceased, it's still hard for a Yorkshire man to resist planting a white rose in his garden!

Roses were prized during the 16th and 17th centuries for their wonderful fragrance. In those days these scented roses would have been the double-flowered cabbage roses, or Centifolias. During this time, roses and rose water were so valued that the nobility considered them legal tender.

Rose breeding

Rose breeding as we know it today began in the late 18th century. *Rosa × odorata* 'Pallida', or the old blush China rose, was brought back from China by the Dutch East India Company in 1781. This was not the showiest of roses, but it repeat flowered from early summer through to autumn. Over the next few years the tea clippers brought back many more China roses which, when

hybridized with the summer-flowering Shrub roses already in cultivation, led to the development of Tea, Bourbon and Portland roses. These had double flowers and scent and, most importantly, repeat flowered – every rose lover's dream.

Probably the most famous rose grower of all time gardened in the late 18th century. This was Empress Josephine, Napoleon's wife. She was a great collector and had around 250 species of rose in her garden at the Château de la Malmaison, just outside Paris. Her roses became the muses of the botanical artist Pierre-Joseph Redouté (1759–1840), who immortalized them in what is considered to be the finest collection

The meaning of colour

Great symbolic significance has been attributed to roses over the years. Different coloured roses mean different things; perhaps it's wise to know this before you choose which one to give. A red rose means love and desire. A white rose, on the other hand, indicates friendship and innocence. Pink roses symbolize elegance and refinement. Yellow roses indicated jealousy in Victorian times, which is perhaps why Algernon rejects the offer of a yellow 'Maréchal Niel' in favour of a pink rose in Oscar Wilde's play *The Importance of Being Earnest*.

The sumptuous beauty of the pink Centifolia rose is perfectly captured by Redouté in *Les Roses*, a collection of botanical paintings, c.1820.

rose. Although we claim that the rose is a quintessentially English flower, up to now its history had belonged to Asia and mainland Europe, and this next leap forward took place in France. A chance seedling of unknown parentage was found by a Frenchman in his garden. This signified the dawn of a new era in the romance of the rose. Not surprisingly, this first Hybrid Tea was named 'La France'.

Modern roses

More recently, in the mid-20th century, a great surge of interest in rose growing led to countless new varieties of Modern Bush roses (Hybrid Teas and Floribundas). New colour breaks, such as the brilliant

vermilion 'Super Star' and the deliciously scented 'Fragrant Cloud', fuelled the demand. Roses were accessible. No longer did you have to order them from the rose nursery; you could buy them in plastic bags or coloured boxes from the local shop or department store, including Woolworths. Rose aficionados planted dedicated beds of new varieties. However, the average plot in 1970s suburbia would have sported a collection of ill-matched varieties amassed over a number of years, including 'Masquerade', 'Queen Elizabeth', 'Lili Marlene' and of course the best-loved Hybrid Tea of all time: 'Peace'.

The roses we filled our gardens with quickly became fair game for

of botanical illustrations ever painted. Was he inspired by the roses or by the Empress? We'll never know. Legend has it that when Napoleon departed for Waterloo, Josephine presented him with a beautiful, pale pink Bourbon rose saying, 'Take this as a souvenir de la Malmaison'. The rose that carries this name is still grown today – a temperamental beauty that likes her creature comforts, just like Josephine.

Josephine is also attributed with a certain style of rose garden: beds devoted purely to roses, usually consisting of one or two varieties. This way of growing roses has lasted and, although we grow roses in lots of different ways today, the dedicated rose bed has survived in gardens for the past 200 years.

The mid-19th century saw the introduction of the first Hybrid Tea

Today we tend to use roses in mixed borders, growing in harmony with other shrubs, perennials and annuals, rather than planting them in dedicated rose beds.

pests and diseases that did not have to search too far to find hosts. Black spot and mildew moved in with a vengeance, particularly after the ban on coal fires in 1956, as diseases spread more rapidly in clean air. The quest for a miracle cure began, and still goes on. However, nowadays we understand the importance of growing disease-resistant varieties, and how good gardening practice helps to combat pests and diseases more successfully than a regime of using pesticides and other chemicals.

Recent years have seen a change in the way we garden. The range of plant material available to the gardener has never been greater, and our approach to gardening is more informal than it used to be. Rather than simply growing roses on their own, in dedicated beds, we often plant them in borders combined with other shrubs and perennials. This type of planting demands a different kind of rose – one that enjoys the company of other plants. The old-fashioned Shrub rose suits mixed plantings, but often flowers only once and is sometimes not of strong enough constitution to stand up to our less attentive approach to the garden. The English rose fits the bill (*see* pages 18 and 88–92), combining the best attributes of ancient and modern while retaining the essence and beauty of the rose.

(see pages 18 and 88–92)

Don't forget

When you visit a rose garden, take a notebook and a camera with you. You could photograph the roses with their labels, if they have them, so you won't forget your favourites. Remember to look at the whole planting, not just the rose.

Seeking inspiration

There is nothing like seeing a rose 'in the flesh' to help you decide whether it is the right one to grow in your garden. You can study its size, habit and flower power, and see what it looks like combined with other plants. A visit to a rose garden, ideally in early summer, is the best way to do this. Try to visit in the evenings if possible, because both colour and fragrance are at their best at this time of day.

The Alnwick Garden, Northumberland This amazing garden gives the visitor an opportunity to see a very young Grand Garden, containing over 3,000 English, Shrub, Climbing and Rambler roses.

Coughton Court, Warwickshire The National Trust's Tudor manor garden boasts the amazing Rose Labyrinth. Recognized as one of the finest rose gardens in the world, it is planted with over 200 different rose varieties.

David Austin Rose Garden, Albrighton, Wolverhampton (above) These are the rose gardens of David Austin, the rose breeder responsible for the English rose; here you will see a wonderful collection of over 700 different rose varieties in two acres of inspiring settings.

Mottisfont Abbey, Hampshire (right) A National Trust Garden and home to the National Collection of Old Roses, but it also includes Modern Shrub and English roses. In addition, the garden abounds with lovely perennials and is a great place to get ideas on what to grow with roses.

RHS Rosemoor, Devon Rose lovers will delight in both the dedicated rose gardens and the use of roses in mixed plantings. The Queen Mother's Rose Garden showcases modern roses in formal settings. More than 200 varieties of Shrub rose are to be found elsewhere in the gardens.

Other good rose gardens to visit

Queen Mary's Garden, Regents Park, London

RHS Garden Harlow Carr, Harrogate, Yorkshire

RHS Garden Hyde Hall, Chelmsford, Essex

RHS Garden Wisley, Surrey

Royal Botanic Gardens, Kew, Surrey

The Savill Garden, Windsor Great Park, Berkshire

Trentham Gardens, Staffordshire

Wollerton Old Hall, Shropshire

What is a rose?

However limited your knowledge of plants and gardening, the chances are you know what a rose looks like. We all have an image in our minds of the typical rose – the sort we see on a greetings card, a box of chocolates or in the florist's window. But what exactly is a rose?

Roses are perennial plants, surviving from year to year by producing woody stems. Most have a dormant period in winter, when growth slows down and flowering stops; usually the leaves fall, although a few semi-evergreen varieties retain most of their foliage. In warmer climates roses can behave differently, and even the deciduous types remain evergreen and continue to grow and flower all year.

Some roses grow as shrubs, producing a number of stems rising from ground level to heights that can be anything from 30cm (12in) to 3m (10ft) or more. Others produce much longer stems and climb or scramble over anything that will provide support. Most roses have thorny stems, particularly those in the wild that scramble through hedges and up trees. However, some garden roses have much smoother stems and are a lot less prickly.

Garden roses are the result of years of breeding and selection, and bear little resemblance to their wild ancestors. It is rose breeding that is responsible for the amazing range of colours, flower forms and fragrances we find in our gardens today.

Beauty and fragrance

Roses are grown primarily for their blooms. Many produce only one major flush of flowers in early summer, while others repeat flower, or bloom almost continuously through summer and into autumn.

Number of petals

Roses are single, semi-double or double, depending on the number of petals.

SINGLE
Species roses and some cultivars (here, 'Francis E. Lester') have single flowers with fewer than 8 petals.

SEMI-DOUBLE
Semi-double roses (here, 'Queen Mother') have between 8 and 20 petals in two or three rows.

DOUBLE
Double roses have over 20 petals (here, 'Scepter'd Isle'). Fully double varieties have over 30 petals.

Arrangement of flowers on the stem

The way in which rose flowerheads are carried on their stems varies according to the type of rose. They may be solitary, sometimes with two or more buds behind the main flower, or grouped in clusters or sprays.

SOLITARY
A single flower is carried at the end of each stem, as with many Hybrid Teas.

CLUSTER
Several flowers arise from a single, often upright stem, as with Floribundas.

SPRAY
A profusion of smaller flowers is borne on a lax, single stem, as with Ramblers.

The flowers vary considerably in number of petals, flower shape, and how they are carried on the stem.

Some roses produce attractive fruits, known as hips, when the flowers fade. They may be round, oval or bottle-shaped, in red, orange or brown, and can have as much ornamental value as the flowers.

Rose leaves are made up of several leaflets arranged on a leaf-stalk and range in colour from light apple green to very dark green flushed with purple. The new foliage is often flushed copper or red as it unfurls.

One of the main reasons gardeners grow roses is because of their fragrance. This scent can be heavy, light, fresh, fruity or spicy. Some roses have a real old-rose fragrance while others smell of tea, myrrh or lemon. To some extent, fragrance is subjective, so what one gardener considers delightful, another may consider insignificant.

Flower shapes

Roses come in a range of shapes. Below are some of the most distinctive double forms.

HIGH-CENTRED
A tall, tight centre is typical of a Hybrid Tea.

POMPON
Small and rounded with lots of regularly arranged petals.

ROSETTE
Fairly flat, with many short, often overlapping petals.

QUARTERED
Almost flat and seems to be divided into four sections.

RECURVED
Petals arch backwards, giving an 'open' appearance.

INCURVED
Petals bend inwards, giving a 'closed' appearance.

Growth habits of roses

Roses are very varied in habit, but they fall loosely into three main growth types: bushy, arching and upright. Shrub roses (including English roses) can be bushy, arching or upright; Modern Bush roses are usually bushy or upright; Climbing and Rambler roses tend to have arching or upright stems; Patio roses are bushy; and Ground-cover roses have arching, ground-hugging stems.

BUSHY HABIT
A rounded to spreading form, with a relatively dense centre.

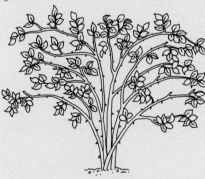
ARCHING HABIT
Stems spread outwards and, in the case of some Ground-cover roses, downwards.

UPRIGHT HABIT
Strong, stiff, erect stems that grow vertically rather than horizontally.

Rose types and uses

There are so many different types of rose. Their diversity in flower form and colour means that there's one that is sure to please for just about every garden situation, including neat, compact varieties that grow in pots on the patio, large, bushy shrubs for borders, climbing types that make their way up a wall or a pergola, and vigorous varieties that scramble through the tallest trees. Some roses seem happier planted with their own kind, while others are more gregarious creatures that mix happily with shrubs and perennials.

Shrub roses

This is a loose umbrella term for a large and diverse group of roses that vary in habit from small, bushy shrubs growing to around 1m (40in) in height and spread to sizeable, arching shrubs reaching three or four times that size. The group includes the garden-worthy species (wild) roses, old garden roses that have been grown for hundreds of years, and many more recent introductions. As with any other flowering shrub, roses in this group generally cohabit well with other roses or shrubs in mixed borders.

Some Shrub roses – particularly the old-fashioned types – flower only once, in early summer, while others (including Ground-cover roses and English roses) repeat flower. For more information on types of Shrub rose and individual cultivars, *see* pages 16–17 and 80–92.

Summer-flowering varieties

Despite their lack of repeat performance, these beautiful old roses possess a subtle charm that earns them a place in today's

'Charles de Mills' is an elegant, highly fragrant, summer-flowering Shrub rose that looks magnificent in a mixed border.

gardens and in the heart of many a gardener. A great number of them are wonderfully fragrant. They have pleasingly flattened double flowers, their petals often crimped into an intricate rosette or gathered into quarters. They can be richly coloured, like the dark crimson 'William Lobb'. He is a tall aristocrat for the back of the border, while the deep-purple 'Tuscany Superb' is a gem to savour closer at hand. Some have intricately formed buds, like those of *Rosa × centifolia* 'Cristata' (formerly 'Chapeau de Napoléon'), whose textured calyces earn it the common name crested moss rose. Sometimes the colour of summer-flowering varieties is more intense in the depths of the bloom, fading to more subtle shades.

Repeat-flowering varieties

As rose breeding progressed, breeders developed Shrub roses that bloomed more than once in a season, some with great continuity. They were understandably popular, and many of these earlier varieties have stood the test of time, despite the introduction of thousands of new varieties over recent years.

Don't forget

Planting summer-flowering roses with later-flowering perennials, such as achilleas, salvias and asters, helps to extend the season. Try growing small, late-flowering clematis through mature Shrub roses to add colour when the rose blooms fade.

Flower Carpet roses produce a continuous show of blooms throughout the season and are undemanding.

The Bourbon roses have remained popular for their double, fragrant blooms. Like many Bourbons, the glorious 'Madame Isaac Pereire', which dates from the mid-19th century, has a lax habit but it can be grown as a beautiful climber and has deep-pink flowers with a wonderful scent. Another good, old-fashioned repeat-flowering rose is 'Madame Knorr' (formerly 'Comte de Chambord'), with lovely, double, pink, strongly scented blooms carried on a short, compact plant. 'Ferdinand Pichard' is another enduring variety, with mauve-pink, fragrant blooms that are boldly striped crimson-purple. It has been attracting attention in gardens for nearly 90 years.

Ground-cover roses

Some repeat-flowering Shrub roses form mounds or even sprawl over a wide area of ground. These can be used as effective ground cover on sunny banks or even at the front of large beds and borders.

The Flower Carpet roses have become very popular in recent

'Madame Knorr' flowers almost all summer long and is a lovely choice for a small garden.

Don't forget

Regular dead-heading of repeat-flowering Shrub roses encourages further flowers and keeps plants tidy. Look for where a new shoot is emerging behind the existing flowerhead and cut just above it (see pages 58–9 and 76).

years. These are free-flowering over a long period and have shiny, disease-resistant foliage. They form lax mounds of stems and need little attention apart from the occasional tidy-up with a pair of shears in spring. The original 'Flower Carpet Pink' has now been joined by a whole spectrum of other colours.

Glossary of Shrub rose types

There are many different types of Shrub rose. You don't want to get bogged down with these terms, but it can be useful as well as interesting to know a little about the background of rose types, because understanding their origin is likely to give an indication of common characteristics, cultivation requirements and uses. English roses are described on page 18.

ALBA

This is an ancient group thought to be derived from *Rosa damascena* and *R. canina*. The habit is upright, the foliage blue-grey and striking, and the semi-double to double blooms, which appear in a single flush in summer, are delicate and fragrant. Albas are tolerant and relatively disease-resistant. *R. × alba* 'Alba Semiplena' (left) is one of the oldest of all Albas.

BOURBON

Bourbons came into being in about 1817, after a chance cross between the Autumn Damask and the old blush China rose on the Île de Bourbon (Réunion Island), in the Indian Ocean. They have double or fully double, fragrant flowers in flushes in summer and autumn, and can be trained to climb. 'Madame Isaac Pereire' (left) is a justly popular Bourbon.

CENTIFOLIA

Derived from the cabbage or Provence rose, and popular in the 17th century, these have double or fully double, often fragrant flowers that appear in one flush in summer. Although beautiful, they are not very pest- or disease-resistant, and have a lax habit so need supporting. 'Robert le Diable' (left) has neat, purple flowers splashed with cerise.

CHINA

The old blush China rose (*Rosa × odorata* 'Pallida', left), which came to Europe from China in the late 18th century, is the ancestor of modern repeat-flowering roses. This rose is still grown, as are various hybrids. China roses are single to double, borne in clusters, and are sometimes fragrant. There are both bushy and climbing types available.

DAMASK

Grown mainly for their intense fragrance, most Damasks, including 'Celsiana' (left), flower in a single flush in summer and derive from *R. damascena*. The blooms are semi-double to double. There are also some repeat-flowering varieties, derived from the Autumn Damask, which was important in rose breeding in the 19th century.

GALLICA

Some of the oldest roses are in this group, including the apothecary's rose (*Rosa gallica* var. *officinalis*) and *R. gallica* 'Versicolor' (left). They are derived from the wild rose *R. gallica* – one of the main ancestors of modern roses. Gallicas are normally compact, with single to fully double flowers in summer; they are usually tolerant of poor soil.

HYBRID MUSK

This is a group of vigorous, repeat-flowering roses that emerged in the early 20th century, yet have the informal charm of the old, summer-flowering Shrub roses. They produce a profusion of mainly double blooms, borne in large clusters, and usually have a distinctive scent. 'Felicia' (left) has healthy foliage and delicate, creamy-pink flowers.

HYBRID PERPETUAL

These tall, upright, repeat-flowering roses were popular in the 19th century and many are still grown today, including 'Ferdinand Pichard' (left). However, their popularity waned when their offspring, the Hybrid Teas, were created, as these have a neater, more compact habit. The flowers tend to be red or pink, fully double and often fragrant.

MOSS

This group of intriguing roses, derived from a Centifolia and an Autumn Damask, is named for the aromatic, moss-like growth on the stem and just below the sepals. The semi-double to fully double flowers are usually scented and some varieties are repeat-flowering. The crested moss rose (*Rosa × centifolia* 'Cristata', right) is a summer-flowering variety.

SCOTS

These low, spreading roses, all derived from the Burnet rose (*Rosa spinosissima*), were popular in the early 19th century. They have prickly stems and single to double flowers that bloom for a short time. In the 20th century, they were crossed with Hybrid Teas for longer flowering. 'Stanwell Perpetual' (right) is the most widely grown Scots rose.

NOISETTE

The Noisettes came into being in the 19th century, when an old blush China rose (*see* opposite) was crossed with a musk rose (*R. moschata*) to produce fragrant, repeat-flowering varieties, such as 'Noisette Carnée' (right). Most are white, cream or pale pink. Noisettes tend to be large with lax stems and so are best grown as climbers.

SWEET BRIAR

Initially bred from the eglantine rose, or sweet briar (*Rosa rubiginosa*, right) in the 19th century, these vigorous, free-branching, thorny bushes are excellent for hedging. The usually single blooms are fragrant, borne in summer and followed by hips in autumn. The foliage of the species and some of its varieties has a wonderful, apple-like scent.

POLYANTHA

Popular in the late 19th century, these compact roses produce sprays of single to double flowers in flushes in summer and autumn. They are very colourful and hardy, but the blooms are small and rarely fragrant. Polyanthas were crossed with Hybrid Teas to create Floribundas, which have almost replaced them. 'The Fairy' (right) is still grown today.

TEA

The original Tea rose (*Rosa odorata*) came from China in the 1800s and was crossed with other roses to create fragrant, elegant hybrids with high-centred, semi- to fully double blooms. However, they were not hardy, so they were crossed with the hardier Hybrid Perpetuals to create Hybrid Teas. 'Gloire de Dijon' (right) is a Climbing Tea rose.

PORTLAND

In the late 18th century, a chance cross between a Gallica rose and an Autumn Damask resulted in the first Portland rose. More cultivars were developed when this was crossed with China roses. Portlands are upright, compact and repeat-flowering, with semi- to fully double blooms that are often scented, such as 'Marchesa Boccella' (right).

SPECIES

Most of the roses we grow in our gardens are the results of extensive breeding and cultivation and have come a long way from their wild rose ancestors. However, there are a number of roses, including *Rosa primula* (right), that are much closer to their roots, so to speak. Known as species roses, these are either just as they would grow in the wild or are selections or hybrids that retain the basic characteristics of the species. Usually known by their Latin name, most are hardy characters with great charm. They usually produce single blooms in one flush in early summer and are followed by colourful hips, which can be even more of a feature than the flowers. Species roses can be magnets for bees and other pollinating insects.

RUGOSA

These tough modern roses, derived from the Japanese rose *Rosa rugosa*, have upright, very thorny stems. All repeat flower, have disease-free, heavily veined foliage, fragrant blooms and are very tolerant. The single varieties, such as *R. rugosa* 'Alba' (right), produce attractive, large, tomato-like hips. Some varieties are semi-double or double.

English roses

While the purists may stick with the classic old, summer-flowering roses, many gardeners today prefer to grow the English roses. These are the work of rose breeder David Austin and combine the charm and flower form of the old Shrub roses with the repeat-flowering quality, reliability and disease-resistance of many modern varieties. English roses also have a much wider colour range than the old roses, as well as delicious perfumes, new flower forms and versatile growth habits.

These are real garden roses that fit in anywhere. All look glorious in a mixed border and they will also satisfy the enthusiast who wants a dedicated rose garden. Some are very suitable for pots; others can be grown as controllable climbers.

Some of the earlier varieties were rather tall, with a tendency to produce vigorous shoots reaching several feet in the air, stranding the flowers well above eye level. 'Heritage', for example, has beautiful pale pink flowers with incurved shiny petals, but when these are carried

on upright stems 2m (6ft) or more in height it's difficult to appreciate them. Even the popular golden-yellow 'Graham Thomas' can be guilty of having an ungainly habit. However, many more recent rose introductions, for example 'Jubilee Celebration', are bushier and more compact, producing abundant shoots and therefore more flowers.

English roses grown as climbers

The vigorous growth of some English rose varieties can be harnessed and used to the gardener's advantage. For example, the pale pink 'The Generous Gardener', and the peachy-pink 'A Shropshire Lad' (above) make excellent climbers clothed in flowers from tip to toe when well grown. Their tidy habit makes them ideal for a small garden, especially for growing up archways, on obelisks and around the front door.

Don't forget

English roses make wonderful cut flowers, especially the most fragrant ones. The deep-pink 'Gertrude Jekyll' and rich magenta-purple 'Young Lycidas' will fill a room with their gorgeous scent. Their informal but opulent air suits simple arrangements in bowls or vases.

'Golden Celebration' is one of the finest English roses, with an elegant, arching habit and large, deliciously fragrant, double blooms.

Modern Bush roses

These roses, which became popular in the mid-20th century, include the Hybrid Teas, sometimes called Large-flowered Bush roses; Floribundas, often called Cluster-flowered Bush roses; Patio roses, which are more compact Floribundas; and Miniature roses, which are tiny versions of Patio roses. All repeat flower from early summer through to early autumn. For information on individual cultivars, *see* pages 93–101.

Hybrid Tea roses

The Hybrid Tea rose is everyone's idea of the archetypal rose. Typically pointed buds open to double, often high-centred flowers with gently unfurling petals. In most cases, large, individual flowers are carried on strong stems, but there are often two or more secondary buds behind the primary bloom. Healthy plants have bold, glossy foliage, often bronze near the tips of the shoots. Fragrance can be strong or light, and typically there is a distinct smell of tea somewhere in the complex notes of that scent. This comes from one of the parents – a delicate Tea rose that was crossed with a repeat-flowering Hybrid Perpetual

rose – hence the name Hybrid Tea, often abbreviated to HT. Roses in this group tend to have distinct flushes of blooms in summer and autumn rather than the continuous display of the Floribundas.

Hybrid Teas have, for many years, been regarded as the most popular type of rose. They're suitable for beds and borders, particularly narrower ones because their size can be controlled regularly, and they're also excellent for cutting and for showing. Today, they've lost some of their popularity to English roses and Floribundas, which usually have a more informal habit, are better mixers with other shrubs and perennials, and tend to be hardier,

'Julia's Rose' is an elegant Hybrid Tea in intriguing shades of coffee, copper and pink. Its unusual colouring and upright stems make it popular with flower arrangers.

Don't forget

If you crave the classic red rose in your garden, look to the Hybrid Teas, such as 'Alec's Red' and 'Royal William'.

'Silver Jubilee' is, justifiably, one of the most popular Hybrid Tea roses because of its compact growth and continuous, free-flowering habit.

'Arthur Bell' is a reliable Floribunda with bright yellow, fragrant blooms that are produced in large clusters.

'Trumpeter' is a compact, free-flowering, brilliant red Floribunda that remains disease-free all season.

more tolerant of wet and easier to care for. However, Hybrid Teas are still very popular as anniversary gifts and many have been named to make them appropriate for milestone wedding anniversaries, birthdays and other events.

There is a great range of colours, from the most pure and subtle to the richly intense, so they offer enormous possibilities for creative colour combinations.

Floribundas

The word 'Floribunda' means lots of flowers, and that's what you'll get from this lovely group of roses. First produced in the 1920s, they're available in a fantastic range of colours and they bloom almost continually throughout summer and autumn. The flowers are produced in large clusters on strong, upright stems, rather than as individual blooms like the Hybrid Teas. Although the flowers of Floribundas are smaller than those of the Hybrid Teas, their abundance and frequency of flowering means that they make a huge impact. Early varieties lacked the fragrance of the Hybrid Teas, but some more recent introductions rival them for fragrance. The lovely white 'Margaret Merril', for example, has

Don't forget

Floribunda roses often have bold, strong colouring and so are ideal for hot schemes combined with other brightly coloured plants, such as crocosmias, heleniums and rudbeckias.

'Iceberg' is ideal for a mixed border combined with other shrubs, climbers (here, clematis) and perennials.

a wonderful scent and high-centred blooms like those of a Hybrid Tea.

Floribundas are often used in the same way as Shrub roses. Although you can grow them on their own in a rose bed, they are good mixers, combining well with shrubs and perennials; some of the more vigorous, bushy varieties are suitable for informal hedges or for the back of a border. Although many have bold, bright blooms (red, yellow and orange tend to predominate), there are plenty of more subtle shades on offer. For instance, the lovely 'Iceberg', with its pure white blooms and apple-green foliage, is a garden classic that will be at home in any white garden or pale colour scheme.

Patio roses

Very compact Floribunda varieties are known as Patio roses. Generally easy to grow, these are usually about 30–60cm (12–24in) or so high, have a bushy habit and are very useful in small gardens, narrow borders and patio containers. As they're often sold as containerized plants in bloom, they're a great way of adding colour during the summer season. Most repeat flower well and will reward year after year. Patio roses are also grown as standards on stems around 1m (40in) high (*see* pages 64–5). These can be an eye-catching way to add focal points to a summer bedding scheme or as colourful statements in a pot on the patio.

There are also climbing Patio roses, ideal for small gardens and containers. These are slender, small-leaved varieties with light growth and small flowers produced freely over a long season.

'Warm Welcome' is one of the most popular climbing Patio roses, with its dark green, purple-tinged leaves and glowing orange flowers.

Miniature roses

Miniature roses are even smaller than Patio roses, and are delicate little creatures with tiny blooms on plants that rarely reach 30cm (12in). They are not very robust and seem to dislike root disturbance, hence their lack of popularity. They are often sold as house plants and sometimes, if planted out in the garden in spring, they can become a permanent feature. Where they succeed, Miniature roses are charming little plants that are ideal for growing in small gardens and containers on the patio.

'Étoile de Hollande' is a magnificent rich-red, repeat-flowering Climbing rose. It has a strong, sweet scent.

Climbing roses

The growth habits of Climbing roses vary greatly. Some are very upright in habit and lend themselves to high walls or fences, or the uprights of large pergolas, rather than training along lower fences or up a small arch. For example, 'Madame Alfred Carrière' has very upright, almost thornless stems and slender shoots. She may look like a delicate creature, but she is actually a strong grower and does not respond well to being trained horizontally.

For a lower wall, or to grow up a stout post as a pillar rose, the English rose 'The Pilgrim' would be an excellent choice. This can be

Don't forget

Although most Climbing roses are repeat-flowering, few cultivars bloom truly continuously throughout the season, so it's a good idea to combine them with clematis, honeysuckle or other appropriate climbers to fill the gaps (see pages 42–3).

Climbing and Rambler roses

Climbing and Rambler roses both have long stems and need some form of support. They differ in several ways (*see* right). However, many new varieties have been developed as a result of years of interbreeding and these differences are not as clear-cut as they once were. To add to the confusion, some Shrub roses, including English roses, and several Modern Bush rose varieties, can be grown and trained as climbers or wall shrubs.

What's the difference?

CLIMBING ROSES	RAMBLER ROSES
Less vigorous, more controllable growth than Ramblers	Very strong-growing, natural scramblers
More erect growth than Ramblers, on arching, stiff stems	Long, arching, sometimes lax canes, almost like blackberries
Larger flowers than Ramblers, more like Hybrid Tea, Floribunda or Shrub roses, borne either singly or in small clusters	Smaller flowers produced in larger sprays, sometimes up to 21 blooms per stem, carried at the tips of the stems
Most repeat flower	Most bloom only once, in early summer
Appreciate a little more care and attention than Ramblers and really need annual pruning and training. Prune quite lightly immediately after flowering, rather like a Shrub rose (see pages 61–2)	Ramblers cope with neglect, but will become a bit unkempt and unmanageable after a few years. Prune after flowering, usually in late summer, and hard prune every few years (see pages 62–3)
Ideal for average-sized fences and walls, trellis outside the front door, and garden structures, e.g. small arches, arbours, obelisks; good for smaller, tidier gardens	Will clamber up a tree, drape themselves over a pergola or the roof of a garage or scale a high wall or fence; suited to more naturalistic settings

'Bobbie James' is a giant of a Rambler, with sprays of creamy-white, scented flowers borne in profusion in early summer and orange hips in autumn. It has a lovely, natural beauty and looks stunning scrambling up a large tree or over a building.

grown as a shrub, but its tall, upright habit makes it ideal to grow as a short climber, reaching up to 2–3m (6–10ft) in height.

For an archway or an arbour, or to train around a front door, the ever-popular 'New Dawn' would be perfect. This has glossy, dark green foliage, pale pink flowers produced freely throughout the summer, and pliable shoots that are easily trained to follow whichever direction the gardener desires.

Rambler roses

The most vigorous Rambler roses are perfect to grow through trees or over pergolas. 'Paul's Himalayan Musk' is one of the finest, with its large clusters of soft-pink, double flowers with their heavy and delicious perfume. The long, pliable stems will grow to 10m (33ft) or more, and once it gets going there's no stopping it.

'Félicité Perpétué', on the other hand, grows only to 5m (16ft) or so and has slender stems, almost evergreen leaves and a bushy habit. The hanging clusters of creamy,

Don't forget

Most Rambler roses flower only once, in early to midsummer. To extend the season, plant later-flowering *Clematis viticella* varieties to grow through them. These come into their own from midsummer onwards, producing an abundant display of small, colourful flowers.

pink-tinged pompon flowers are at their best when hanging from the rafters of a low pergola or broad arch. This is also a lovely rose to grow along a rope slung between stout posts at the back of a border.

For further suggestions of how and where to grow Climbing and Rambling roses against supports, *see* pages 52–6 and 110–23. For detailed information on individual cultivars, *see* pages 102–9.

FOCUS ON | Roses for cutting

Of course, your roses look wonderful in the garden, but it's also one of life's great pleasures to cut a few to bring indoors – maybe to decorate the dinner table, to have alongside you at your desk, or to put in the bedroom so that you go to sleep with their fragrance and awake with it in the morning. For a rose lover, these cut flowers never seem to last long enough. However, if you follow a few simple guidelines there are ways of extending the life of roses in the home.

Double roses are ideal for cutting and look lovely in simple vases.

① Gather roses when the blooms are just opening if you want them to last as long as possible.

② Just a single rose bloom (here, 'New Dawn') can fill a room with its sweet fragrance.

Types of roses for cutting

Hybrid Tea roses particularly lend themselves to cutting. As there is often only one main flower on a stem, you won't be losing subsequent blooms by cutting them. English roses also make good cut flowers and are lovely crowded into a simple vase or a jug as a loose, relaxed posy. Single-flowered roses are not ideal for cutting, unless you want them for very short-term decoration; they rarely last more than a day or two. Those that produce hips, however, are lovely to cut when in fruit for autumn arrangements.

When to cut roses

Opinions vary on the best time to cut roses. Some say early in the morning, when the flowers are cool and the plants have had the opportunity to take up water overnight. Others say in the evening, when their food content is at its highest after a day in the sun. The main thing is to avoid cutting at the hottest time of the day, when the flowers are limp and warm. If this is unavoidable, put the roses straight into water and stand them somewhere cool to condition them before arranging.

Ideally, choose roses where the buds are just starting to unfurl or the bloom is newly opened. However, fully open roses removed as part of the dead-heading process still have a life in a vase for a day or two.

How to cut roses

The length of stem you cut will depend on the flower. The shorter the stem, the less distance the water has to travel to the flower. Large, double-flowered Shrub roses, which can have fine stems, tend to last better when cut short, while Hybrid Tea roses succeed on longer stalks, because the heads are less likely to bend over, blocking the vessels that carry water. Always cut them with a sharp pair of bypass secateurs, which will not crush the stems. Make a clean, diagonal cut above a node – that is, where the leaf meets the stem (see page 57).

Preparing roses for the vase

Remove the lower leaves and thorns that will be below water to prevent rotting. Nifty little gadgets are available to do this, and some people may recommend running a half-open pair of scissors or secateurs down the

Don't forget

Place arrangements in a cool place, out of direct sunlight – the warmer it is, the faster the roses will deteriorate.

Shrub roses are charming in an informal arrangement with other garden flowers.

stems. However, both methods damage the stem and can reduce the plant's ability to take up water. It is far better to employ a little patience and do it by hand.

Plunge the cut stems straight into a clean vase of fresh water, ideally containing a cut-flower nutrient, available from florists, garden centres and some supermarkets. Aspirin, sugar, pennies, bleach, lemon juice or any of the other 'magical' ingredients don't work. Avoid using softened water, as this can affect the life of the flowers.

If you can't put your roses into water straight away, recut the stems above the next node when you put them into a vase.

Roses suitable for cutting

'Alec's Red'	'Molineux'
'Elina'	'Ophelia'
'Elizabeth Harkness'	'Pascali'
	'Royal William'
'Gertrude Jekyll'	'Savoy Hotel'
'Golden Celebration'	'Simply the Best'
	'The Pilgrim'
'Graham Thomas'	'Valencia'
'Just Joey'	'Velvet Fragrance'

Other uses for roses in the home

Roses can be used in many other ways in the home. If you want to dry them, cut them in their prime and hang them upside down in a warm, airy place until completely dry. They will then hold on to petals and colour. For pot-pourri, gather petals when the blooms are fully open and spread them out on absorbent paper or linen on trays in a well-ventilated, warm place until the petals dry completely. If you have difficulty air drying certain roses, try using a dessicant such as silica gel. Rose petals can also be used in the kitchen in jams, preserves and infusions and for decorative purposes too, particularly when the petals are crystallized.

Arranging short-stemmed roses

Some roses grow naturally on very short stems and these tend to topple out of a vase when you put them in water. In this case, make a simple noughts and crosses lattice out of sticks or thin canes that will sit neatly above a bowl of water. Add a few dark green leaves and arrange the rose heads on the lattice so that their faces can be seen and their stems are immersed in the water. They will last well arranged in this way and you will see their beauty. Alternatively, you could use florist's foam. Make sure you soak it thoroughly before use and let it sink to the bottom of the container (rather than push it down) before carefully inserting the stems.

Growing roses with other plants

At one time, roses were grown on their own, in dedicated rose beds. However, today most of us grow roses in mixed borders with other shrubs, perennials and maybe a few annuals and bulbs for seasonal colour. This has two main advantages: to enhance the beauty of the roses when they're in bloom, and to extend the season. Even roses that repeat flower during summer have their 'off' moments, so other plants can step in and fill the gaps. Ideally, we also want colour and interest among the roses in spring before they start to bloom, and through autumn and winter when they rest.

General considerations

When planning a mixed border containing roses, your first consideration should be the size and habit of the rose in relation to the width of the planting area. It's no good planting a beautiful, fragrant variety if it looks uncomfortable and out of scale in its surroundings. Roses vary greatly in size and shape, so choose one to suit the space available, then select planting companions to enhance the scheme throughout the year.

Shrub roses, perennials and clematis create a rich combination of colour and texture in a mixed border.

Right rose, right place

In small gardens, where borders are only 1m (40in) or so wide, choose compact roses of upright habit rather than larger, spreading or arching shrubs. Look to the more compact Floribundas, Patio roses and smaller-growing English roses.

In larger planting areas, more than 2m (6ft) wide, you'll get greater impact from your roses by planting less vigorous varieties in threes; these will grow together to look like one large shrub (see page 48). This suits roses of round, bushy or low, spreading habit, including Modern Bush roses and some English roses, such as 'Darcey Bussell' and 'Lady Hamilton'.

Larger-growing Shrub roses are usually best planted individually and positioned further back in the border. This shows off their blooms to greatest advantage and gives the opportunity to plant shrubs for foliage interest in front of them to hide the lower stems of the rose. Some of the summer-flowering Shrub roses are also a good choice here; although they flower only once, you can extend the season by planting perennials in front or by growing clematis through them. Try not to confine all the tall roses to the back of the border. Bring some of them forward into the front half of

a wide border. This will give the planting depth and variety and draw attention to the rose.

Roses with other plants

In mixed borders, the effect is always more pleasing if there is plenty of variety in form and texture. If you choose compact, bushy roses, soften them with light, airy shrubs and perennials. Loose, arching Shrub roses benefit from underplanting with low, mound-forming foliage shrubs and perennials. Drift spike-flowering annuals and perennials through the border to add light height; this veils the colour of some of the more intense flowers as you look at them, adding depth and interest to the planting.

Avoid combining roses with vigorous shrubs and perennials, otherwise you'll have problems with disease because of a lack of air circulation between the plants. Also, as roses are greedy feeders and need moisture at their roots during the growing season, they'll suffer from the competition. Remember to allow

access to the roses for maintenance: don't fill the space so completely that you have to fight your way through and trample on the companion plants in the process.

Roses for mixed borders

NARROW BORDERS
'Brave Heart'
'Queen of Sweden'
'Sweet Dream'
'The Mayflower'
'Trumpeter'
'William Shakespeare 2000'

BACK OF LARGE BORDERS
Rosa × *alba* 'Alba Semiplena'
'Crown Princess Margareta'
'Graham Thomas'
'Königin von Dänemark'
'Maiden's Blush'
'William Lobb'

Don't forget

If you plant dwarf bulbs and early perennials among roses, remember to keep a circle 60cm (2ft) or more completely clear around the base of the rose to allow you to add compost, manure and rose food on a regular basis.

Filling the gaps in winter and spring

Before roses come into leaf, the ground beneath them is clearly visible. This is when early perennials and bulbs take centre stage, bringing a dull border to life. They cover bare earth, flowering in the shade of deciduous plants before the canopy thickens, and can also serve a practical purpose, preventing weeds from taking over. Later, shrubs and perennials can be used to fill the gaps between roses.

Primulas, bugle (*Ajuga*) and pulmonarias create a colourful carpet beneath roses that will come into their own later in the season. A rope swag in the foreground will later be covered in Rambler roses, creating a colonnade (*see* pages 55 and 115).

Perennials for winter and early-spring interest

There are plenty of perennials that will enliven a border in winter and early spring, before the roses produce leaves, and will also help to divert the eye from unsightly rose stems. All of the plants listed here will go with all types of roses.

Hellebores (*Helleborus* × *hybridus*) are excellent for combining with roses. They have nodding, open flowers on 30cm (12in) stems that open in late winter and early spring, and attractive evergreen foliage that lasts through the summer months. Planted as young plants in autumn or winter, they quickly clump up and perform admirably in subsequent years. There's a wide range of colours, from white to deepest purple, with spotted, blotched and double flowers as well as singles. They cross-pollinate easily and self-seed, so don't be surprised to find interesting newcomers in years to come. Like roses, hellebores also dislike competition – therefore, plant them at least 45cm (18in) apart.

Pulmonarias, or lungworts, are also good among roses. They make low clumps of large green leaves, which are usually spotted or marked with silver. In early spring, pretty white, pink, purple or blue flowers appear on 20cm (8in) stems. Some produce pink and blue flowers on the same plant. Pulmonarias are shade-lovers and retain their foliage for most of the year, although this can look tatty in summer; however, once in bloom the roses will hide the leaves. Like pulmonarias, the common primrose (*Primula vulgaris*) and the bright red-purple *Primula*

'Wanda' are both old cottage-garden plants that will self-seed and naturalize themselves among roses and shrubs. These are a delight in early spring and suit informal gardens, either in the town or in the country.

Evergreen heucheras are ideal to grow among roses, even among less vigorous Modern Bush roses, because they make good ground cover around the roses when they bloom as well as being very visible in winter. *Heuchera villosa* 'Palace Purple' was the original foliage heuchera with brown-purple leaves. Apparently, it got its name because it was used as ground cover among the roses at Buckingham Palace. In recent years, many new varieties have been introduced with green, purple, orange and veined foliage. The purple-leaved varieties are the most reliable and useful and look good around roses, especially at the front of the border. *Heuchera* 'Plum Pudding' is one of the best, with wavy, deep-purple leaves with a blotched silver overlay. Tiny white flowers are carried on tall, fine purple stems in summer. Try planting 'Plum Pudding' under pink roses, such as *Rosa* 'Silver Jubilee', as the combination will look wonderful at the height of the season.

Early bulbs

Together with perennials, you can interplant roses with early bulbs. If the soil retains moisture for much of the year, snowdrops (*Galanthus*) will naturalize, their exquisite, small flowers forming a lovely white carpet around the rose's stems. The early *Crocus tommasinianus* and its many varieties also self-seed freely in this situation in some gardens. The slender lilac flowers of the species start to open in late winter and provide welcome colour, sometimes when the snow is still on the

Don't forget

Whatever bulbs you grow among your roses, plant them in clumps rather than singly. They look more natural planted in this way, are easier to manage and have greater impact.

Bulbs make excellent companions for roses, from crocuses, anemones and dwarf narcissi in early spring through to tulips in late spring. Tulips give a fantastic display just before the roses bloom and their leaves die down soon after flowering.

ground. *Anemone blanda* will sometimes naturalize in just the same way, forming clumps of pretty, divided leaves and delighting with its starry blue, pink or white flowers.

Dwarf daffodils, such as *Narcissus* 'February Gold' and the paler yellow-and-white 'Jack Snipe', will add bolder, brighter colour. Larger-flowering varieties are best avoided, as the flowers usually grow up into the branches of the roses and get damaged. You'll also curse the foliage later on, because it takes so long to die down. Dwarf daffodils have finer, shorter leaves and the roses will hide these when they come into leaf.

Don't forget

Tulips don't like heavy, moist soil, so if you're growing roses on clay you may need to replant tulips every year. The bulbs are inexpensive and provide a lot of pleasure for little investment.

Late-spring bulbs

For interest in later spring, tulips are a good choice to grow among roses. Their greatest attribute is that the foliage dies down quickly after flowering, so there are no messy leaves around when the roses are performing. Tulips offer a fantastic range of colour and flower form, so you're bound to find one that will fit in with your colour scheme. Many are more in tune with the rose colour palette than are other spring flowers. The lily-flowering tulips, such as the warm-pink *Tulipa* 'Mariette', are slender and elegant and sit well among other plants. The dark purple tulips, such as 'Queen of Night', work well in any scheme. This is a hardy variety that will appear for several years in most gardens. Avoid large-flowered, gaudy tulips among roses; they're better grown in patio pots.

Camassia leichtlinii is another good choice. This produces a rosette of slender leaves and then a 60cm (2ft) spike of starry blue flowers. It's a lovely addition planted in groups of three to five bulbs, which will increase slowly.

Perennials for late-spring interest

The columbine known as granny's bonnet (*Aquilegia vulgaris*) is a favourite cottage-garden perennial with pretty, fern-like foliage and slender stems carrying distinctive flowers. There are many varieties and the plants set seed easily. Some flowers have long spurs, and there are double and single forms. Choose tall-growing varieties that will grow up through the roses and provide light height in the foreground. The various Barlow aquilegias have double, spurless flowers on tall

Growing bulbs under trained roses

Some Climbing or Rambler roses, or Shrub roses with long, arching stems, can be trained onto hoops of willow or hazel in a wide bed to create a large mound of a shrub with space beneath the branches for planting early-flowering bulbs. This means you'll have an attractive display of flowers before the roses bloom, and as the rose comes into leaf it will hide the bulbs' dying foliage. There are also several practical advantages for the rose: the hooped structure defines the space that the shrub will occupy and keeps it within bounds. Also, by bending the stems over and tying them onto the willow or hazel hoops, you'll encourage the rose to produce more sideshoots and flower more prolifically. You can also grow a clematis through the branches of the rose, which will provide further flowers later in the season.

ROSES TO TRAIN OVER HOOPS
'A Shropshire Lad'
'Albertine'
'Complicata'
'Crown Princess Margareta'
'Madame Isaac Pereire'
'Mortimer Sackler'
'The Pilgrim'
'William Lobb'

To make the supporting structure, first mark out a circle at least 1.5m (5ft) in diameter, then plant the rose in the centre and the bulbs around the edge. Insert long wands of willow or hazel, or heavy but pliable wire, in the ground around the circle's edge and bend them so they form hoops that cross in the centre. As the rose stems grow, tie them into the hoops.

Drifts of columbine (*Aquilegia*) and alliums light up this mixed border before the roses start to bloom. Both will seed themselves freely, creating a wonderfully naturalistic effect.

stems and come in a subtle range of colours that fit into any scheme. *Aquilegia vulgaris* var. *stellata* 'White Barlow' and 'Black Barlow' are stunning with silver foliage plants such as santolina and lavender, both of which are often grown with roses. 'Blue Barlow' is a great mixer, whatever your scheme.

Dicentras, commonly known as bleeding heart, come into their own early in the season and then die down and get out of the way. Varieties such as *Dicentra formosa* 'Langtrees' and *Dicentra* 'Pearl Drops' grow up to 25cm (10in) high, with silver-green, fern-like foliage and delicate stems of pendulous white flowers above the leaves. They work well in any pink or white planting scheme.

Roses are very rounded shrubs, so plants with upright stems contrast well with them and enliven a planting scheme. *Iris sibirica* looks wonderful with roses, and has narrow, upright, gently arching leaves and slender, upright stems carrying exquisite, delicate early flowers. 'Tropic Night' is a good choice, with deep-purple, heavily veined blooms. It's best to avoid planting roses with the bearded flag irises. Although they flower early, they resent competition and don't look good the rest of the season.

Among Shrub roses the common honesty, *Lunaria annua*, with its

bright purple flowers, adds a welcome shot of colour. The plants grow to 80cm (32in) and the flowers fade to produce flattened green pods that turn silver if left in the garden in winter. It's a biennial, so the plant grows one year and flowers the following, then it dies. If you sow seed for two years in succession in the flowering position you should have plants in flower every year thereafter.

Euphorbia characias subsp. *wulfenii* is an excellent architectural plant, with upright stems and heads of lime-green flowers that unfurl in late winter and develop through spring. It's bold and vigorous, growing to

1.2m (4ft), and although it's too heavy to partner most roses, it does look good with yellow English roses, such as 'Graham Thomas' and 'Molineux'. It also helps to extend the season of interest.

Early-flowering shrubs

It's useful to have a few early-flowering shrubs that perform before the first flush of roses appear in early summer. Although many early-flowering shrubs tend to be too overpowering in habit to associate well with roses, there are some that are suitable. The purple-leaved sand cherry (*Prunus × cistena*) is a good choice, with its slight

Camellias and dicentras make a magnificent display in late spring, before roses on this arch come into bloom in early summer. Coordinating the colour in this way maintains the mood of the planting throughout the season.

habit, dark twigs and delicate, pale pink flowers in spring that appear as the plum-purple leaves unfurl. The flowers are a welcome early addition and the foliage works well with the roses later in the season. Also, the fragrant *Viburnum carlesii* and the evergreen *Viburnum tinus* 'Eve Price' are other options, with their pretty, delicate, white flowers that suit the mood of the planting.

Lilacs are a traditional backdrop for roses, but avoid the large-leaved varieties of *Syringa vulgaris*, which are too big for many gardens and add little after the flowers have faded. Instead, choose one of the small-leaved lilacs, which are much more useful. *Syringa meyeri* 'Palibin' has tiny leaves and dainty, fragrant, lilac-pink flowers that appear in late spring. *Syringa* 'Red Pixie' is also excellent. The flowers are deep pink, freely produced and fragrant on a bushy shrub. Both eventually grow to around 1m (40in) in height.

Don't forget

If you're growing more vigorous Shrub and English roses, underplant with stronger-growing ground-cover perennials such as *Alchemilla mollis* and *Symphytum caucasicum*.

Evergreen shrubs

In winter, evergreens form the backbone of the garden and provide much-needed interest in borders. There is a range of foliage colours available, including golden, variegated, silver and purple as well as green, which will provide year-round interest and will also complement the roses when they're in flower (*see* pages 34–5). *Euonymus fortunei* 'Emerald Gaiety', *Buxus sempervirens* 'Elegantissima' and *Osmanthus heterophyllus* 'Variegatus' are just a few evergreen shrubs that look good planted with roses.

Foliage shrubs to grow with roses

Shrubs with attractive leaves are the perfect companions for roses. The foliage enhances the rose blooms while they're performing, and it provides interest when the roses take a break. Purple, silver and variegated shrubs all work well with roses.

Purple and plum foliage

Shrubs with plum or purple foliage are ideal partners for Shrub roses. They break up the flat green of the mature rose leaves, highlight the copper tones of the young foliage and accentuate the colour of the rose blooms. Purple-leaved shrubs add richness and depth, and work with any colour of rose, from pale pink through dark red to gold and orange. They also make a dramatic combination with white roses.

Probably the most useful of all purple foliage shrubs is *Berberis thunbergii* f. *atropurpurea* 'Rose Glow'. It's a small shrub, growing up to 1m (40in) high, with arching branches carrying rounded, red-purple leaves, heavily marbled salmon pink near the tips of the branches. The foliage turns flame red before it falls in late autumn. Its small stature and tough constitution make it ideal to grow among small Shrub roses, such as 'The Mayflower' (*see* right), and shorter Floribundas, including the rich scarlet 'Evelyn Fison'.

Light height really lifts a planting scheme. *Sambucus nigra* f. *porphyrophylla* 'Eva', also known as 'Black Lace', has finely cut, fern-like, dark purple leaves and pale pink flowers in flattened heads in early summer. It grows to 1.5m (5ft), but its lighter structure helps it to mix well with roses, including the deep-purple 'Tuscany Superb' (*see* right), as well as other shrubs, particularly those with silver foliage.

Physocarpus opulifolius 'Diable D'Or' has lovely purplish-bronze foliage, with hints of gold near the tips of the shoots. The tiny flowers mature to clusters of small, dark red, shiny fruits. It is particularly effective with orange and copper Shrub roses, such as the English roses 'Port Sunlight' and 'Lady Emma Hamilton' (*see* right). *Physocarpus opulifolius* 'Diabolo' is larger, growing to 2m (6ft), with dark purple-black leaves.

Berberis thunbergii f. *atropurpurea* 'Rose Glow'

Rosa 'The Mayflower'

Rosa 'Tuscany Superb'

Sambucus nigra f. *porphyrophylla* 'Eva'

Physocarpus opulifolius 'Diable D'Or'

Rosa 'Lady Emma Hamilton'

Other purple and plum shrubs to grow with roses

Berberis × *ottawensis* f. *purpurea* 'Superba'
Cercis canadensis 'Forest Pansy'
Corylus maxima 'Purpurea'
Cotinus coggygria 'Royal Purple'

Cotinus 'Dusky Maiden'
Hebe 'Mrs Winder'
Viburnum sargentii 'Onondaga'
Weigela 'Naomi Campbell'

Don't forget

If you have a really mixed border, including an array of potentially clashing colours, purple foliage shrubs will help to hold the planting scheme together. They particularly complement hot colours.

The purple sage, *Salvia officinalis* 'Purpurascens', is one of the most useful plants you can grow at the front of a border on well-drained soil. It forms a soft mound of foliage, which becomes richer in summer and greyer in winter, and grows quickly from a young plant to form a mound 60cm (2ft) across by 45cm (18in) high. Spikes of blue flowers rise above the foliage in early summer. This plant is wonderful for hiding lower stems of roses, and the colours of foliage and flowers are perfect with any colour rose you team it with.

Silver and grey foliage

Shrubs with silver foliage are the perfect foil for almost all roses. They are good mixers with any colour scheme, they reflect light, and their leaves are often soft, narrow and fine, so complementing the heavier forms of the roses.

Lavender, with its lovely silver-green foliage, is always a popular choice with roses (*see* page 38). The cotton lavender (*Santolina chamaecyparissus, see* right) has densely packed silver foliage and forms a low, rounded shrub up to 60cm (2ft) in height. It lacks the lightness of lavender, but has brighter foliage and looks good at the edge of a bed of roses (here, the pale pink 'Valentine Heart') and perennials alongside a patio or path. Beware of the bright yellow flowers in summer; these are best clipped off before the buds open.

In larger gardens and wide borders, find room for *Elaeagnus* 'Quicksilver'. This is a tall shrub with gently arching branches, to a height of 2m (6ft) or more, and similar spread. The willow-like leaves are bright silver and the tiny, inconspicuous flowers that appear in early summer are deliciously fragrant. It makes a lovely backdrop for any of the Alba roses, such as glowing pink 'Königin von Dänemark', or the white Floribunda 'Iceberg' (*see* right).

Artemisia 'Powis Castle' makes excellent ground cover beneath roses. It has stunning, feathery, silvery-grey foliage and a compact habit when young, becoming more sprawling with age. It likes full sun and well-drained soil and looks fabulous with pink or rich purple roses, such as 'Young Lycidas' (*see* right).

Rosemary is a highly versatile plant that is at home anywhere in the garden. Its narrow, evergreen leaves and graceful habit lighten heavier foliage and add winter interest. The blue flowers appear in spring, so are welcome colour before the roses start to bloom. *Rosmarinus officinalis* 'Miss Jessopp's Upright' has upward-sweeping branches that will not swamp roses growing alongside, providing both subjects are given a bit of space, planted at least 1m (40in) apart.

Rosa 'Valentine Heart'

Santolina chamaecyparissus

Elaeagnus 'Quicksilver'

Rosa 'Iceberg'

Rosa 'Young Lycidas'

Artemisia 'Powis Castle'

Variegated foliage

Variegated shrubs are a good way to add colour and lift a planting scheme. If you're creating a green-and-white border, white-variegated foliage will maintain the colour scheme throughout the season. The same is true of golden variegations in a yellow border. It's never a good idea to mix yellow and white variegations, as they tend to fight each other.

Yellow-variegated shrubs work only with yellow roses. The golden-variegated evergreen *Euonymus japonicus* 'Chollipo', for example, would work well with the yellow English rose 'Molineux' in a shaded border. Similarly, *Euonymus fortunei* 'Emerald 'n' Gold' makes a sunny combination with the new rose 'Absolutely Fabulous' (*see* right).

Soft white variegations are more versatile than yellow. *Cornus alba* 'Sibirica Variegata' has green-and-white variegated leaves, tinged with pink. It's a good mixer with roses, and the red stems add colour to the border in the winter. Try this dogwood with the deep-pink 'Princess Alexandra of Kent' (*see* right).

For silver-variegated evergreens, look to the pittosporums. These have small leaves and create a light effect. *Pittosporum* 'Garnettii' has soft green-and-silver variegated foliage and makes a good background plant for pink or white roses. *Pittosporum tenuifolium* 'Irene Paterson' is whiter and brighter and combines beautifully with the lovely white English rose *Rosa* 'Claire Austin'.

Green foliage

Evergreen shrubs provide essential structure in the garden and are also the perfect backdrop for roses. However, there are many different shades of green and it's important to choose the right combination of green leaves and rose blooms for maximum impact. For example, dark red roses are better set against light green foliage, such as that of *Pittosporum tenuifolium*, rather than dark green. Yellow, white and light pink roses show up well against any green background, but look particularly luminous against dark foliage, such as that of a yew hedge (*Taxus, see* right). Yellow roses make a fresh and lively partnership with yellow-green leaves, such as those of *Griselinia littoralis*. The small, narrow leaves of *Phillyrea angustifolia* and the neat, dark green foliage of *Myrtus communis* are good planting partners for most roses, while the big, bold leaves of *Fatsia japonica* overpower all roses but those with very large flowers.

Euonymus fortunei 'Emerald 'n' Gold'

Rosa 'Absolutely Fabulous'

Rosa 'Princess Alexandra of Kent'

Cornus alba 'Sibirica Variegata'

Rosa 'Paul's Himalayan Musk' growing over a yew hedge.

Companion plants for roses in bloom

There's no shortage of wonderful plants that flower at the same time as your roses start to perform. These add variety of form and colour to the border and set off the roses beautifully. Light, airy perennials are always a good choice as partners for flowers with bold blooms, such as roses.

Light, airy perennials

Lady's mantle (*Alchemilla mollis*) fits the bill perfectly, with its soft, rounded leaves that appear to transform the morning dew or rainfall into drops of mercury. The foamy, lime-green flowers form a gorgeous carpet around the base of your roses, and they're lovely at the edge of the bed or as ground cover beneath Shrub roses. Lady's mantle looks particularly stunning with the soft apricot-coloured flowers and dark green leaves of *Rosa* 'Buff Beauty' and any midsummer border blues such as *Geranium* × *ibericum*.

Catmint (*Nepeta*) is one of the longest-blooming perennials, flowering from early summer through to autumn. Small, grey-green leaves and feathery, soft-blue flowers make it the ideal partner for roses. *Nepeta* 'Six Hills Giant', which reaches 80cm (32in) high, is ideal planted between bushy roses. Alternatively, choose the low, mound-forming *Nepeta* × *faassenii*

The catmint *Nepeta* 'Six Hills Giant' creates a heavenly blue haze beneath the creamy-yellow flowers of *Rosa* 'Albéric Barbier'.

for the front of a border or the base of an informal hedge planted with the creamy-pink *Rosa* 'Felicia'.

Herbaceous geraniums are among the ultimate mixers in the garden, especially the blue ones. *Geranium* 'Johnson's Blue' is still a favourite, with its finely cut leaves and clear lavender-blue, saucer-shaped flowers. It grows to 30cm (12in) high with a spread of 60cm (2ft), so is ideal in front of your roses with *Alchemilla mollis*. *Geranium* 'Jolly Bee' is a little lower and more spreading in habit, with clear blue, white-eyed flowers that bloom throughout summer. *Geranium* 'Rozanne' is similar. *Geranium psilostemon* is much taller, growing to 90cm (3ft). It's suitable to plant between shorter Shrub roses. The flowers are brilliant magenta with black eyes and are striking with purple-pink roses such as *Rosa* 'Marchesa Boccella' (also known as 'Jacques Cartier').

If you garden on chalk, scented pinks are a must to include near the edge of a bed containing roses. They form a low mound of grey-green leaves and their scented flowers appear just in time to enjoy them with the roses. The various varieties of *Dianthus* × *allwoodii* are widely available and are tough and weather-resistant. *Dianthus* 'Doris' is a classic, with soft salmon-pink flowers, lovely with roses, blue geraniums and catmint (*Nepeta*).

Other good perennials to grow with roses

Astrantia major
Baptisia australis
Centaurea montana
Cephalaria gigantea
Chamerion angustifolium 'Album'
Verbascum chaixii 'Album'
Viola cornuta

Bolder perennials

If you have a weakness for roses, you probably can't resist peonies. These glorious flowers bloom at the same time as the first flush of roses, and make the spectacle even more ravishing. They also like rich, fertile soil and mulching with manure in winter, so are highly compatible. Although the flowering season is short – about three weeks – they do have good foliage, which adds to the border for the rest of the season. *Paeonia lactiflora* 'Bowl of Beauty' is a classic, with its bowl-shaped, glowing pink flowers filled with a mass of small cream petals. *Paeonia lactiflora* 'Duchesse de Nemours' is double, white and fragrant. Peonies look particularly good combined with English roses.

Any perennial that carries its flowers on a spike looks striking among roses. Delphiniums spring to mind, and if you're prepared to put in a bit of effort staking them, and cutting them back after flowering, they're rewarding plants. Most are not long-lived, so be prepared to replace them every couple of years. The Pacific hybrids, which are widely available, are shorter than the very tall Elatum delphiniums and are available in a wide range of colours.

Foxgloves are a dream among Shrub roses. Whether you grow a fancy hybrid or the native *Digitalis purpurea*, they're bound to please. *Digitalis purpurea* 'Sutton's Apricot' is a good choice with copper and orange roses. The white *Digitalis purpurea* f. *albiflora* is lovely with white and pink. These foxgloves are biennials, which means they'll die after flowering, so if they don't self-seed (which they probably will) you'll have to replant. The much smaller *Digitalis lutea* is a perennial, with small, tubular, greenish-yellow flowers on fine, arching 80cm (32in) spikes. It's a wonderful plant to drift through a border and will seed itself on most soils.

The dreamy white spires of the foxglove *Digitalis purpurea* f. *albiflora* and the foamy green flowers of *Alchemilla mollis* make perfect planting companions for Shrub roses.

Annuals with roses

Annuals that you can sow directly into the planting position are a splendid way to add further colour and interest to a mixed border with roses. The secret of success is to make sure that the sowing site is weed-free. It's a good idea to cover the ground with some multipurpose compost, sow your seed thinly and then cover with another layer of compost. This keeps any annual weed seeds away from the surface, making sure they don't have the chance to germinate.

Good annuals to combine with roses include love-in-a-mist, such as *Nigella* 'Miss Jekyll' (*see* right), with fern-like foliage and sky-blue flowers; *Cosmos bipinnatus*, with feathery leaves and large, single flowers in shades of pink, crimson, purple and white; and annual clary (*Salvia viridis* var. *comata*, previously *Salvia horminum*), with spikes of pink, white or dark blue bracts.

Don't forget

Alchemilla mollis seeds and spreads. If you want to prevent this, cut it back as soon as the flowers start to go brown. It will respond with a new flush of leaves and more flowers later in the season.

The deliciously scented *Philadelphus* 'Belle Étoile' makes a wonderful planting partner for the fragrant Rambler rose 'Wedding Day'.

Flowering shrubs

There are many flowering shrubs that go with roses. Generally, the best are summer-flowering shrubs of light and graceful habit, as they won't dominate the rose. The following are suitable for the back of the border or for planting between Shrub roses.

Mock orange (*Philadelphus*) is one of the most fragrant flowering shrubs and is a must for those who love scented flowers. There are double and single varieties and they flower along with the roses in early to midsummer. *Philadelphus* 'Belle Étoile' is one of the best singles, with white petals blotched purple-red at the base. Golden stamens crowd the centre of each flower and the scent is heavy and delicious. The shrub has an elegant, arching habit and looks particularly good with the roses 'Wedding Day' (*see* above left) and 'Roseraie de l'Haÿ'. *Philadelphus* 'Virginal' is the classic double white variety. Plant it with the blue-green foliage and fragrant white flowers of *Rosa × alba* 'Alba Semiplena'.

Most weigelas flower in the main rose season. *Weigela* 'Florida Variegata' has the benefit of cream-and-green variegated foliage as well as pinkish-red, funnel-shaped flowers. It is not as vigorous as some and sits comfortably alongside light or deep-pink roses, such as the double English rose 'Princess Alexandra of Kent'.

Lavender – the perfect partner for roses

Lavender seems the obvious choice to grow with roses (here, *Rosa* 'Harlow Carr'). Both plants like an open, sunny position, although the lavender prefers a drier, lighter soil of lower fertility. However, if the lavender is used around the edge of beds or alongside paved areas it seems to cope. Its silver-green foliage and delicate flower spikes complement the bold blooms and green foliage of the roses. Also, let's not forget that these are two of our favourite fragrances. The narrow-leaved English lavender is the hardiest, and usually lives longest. If you want the best dark blue, compact lavender to plant in front of roses, choose *Lavandula angustifolia* 'Hidcote' (left). It's low enough to use even around Hybrid Tea and Patio roses. 'Munstead' has paler blue flowers; 'Imperial Gem' is also excellent but has more purple flowers.

The butterfly (or French) lavenders are also lovely with roses, but are more suited to informal planting rather than as an edging. *Lavandula pedunculata* subsp. *pedunculata* has short purple flower spikes on upright plants. Each purple flowerhead is topped with butterfly-like bracts, hence the name. It has a long flowering period, from late spring to autumn.

Plants that flourish as roses fade

Later-flowering perennials and shrubs that flower from summer into autumn maintain the interest in a border after summer-flowering Shrub roses have finished, and they fill the gaps when repeat-flowering roses take a break. With a little thought you can create some exciting, hot schemes or really mellow colour combinations that reflect the soft light of late summer and autumn.

Later-flowering perennials

Later- and repeat-flowering geraniums are an obvious choice for teaming with roses. The varieties of *Geranium × oxonianum* bloom for a long period, producing several flushes of starry pink flowers. They are strong-growing, to 80cm (32in) high, so are useful among Shrub roses, English roses and taller Floribundas. *Geranium × oxonianum* 'A.T. Johnson' is popular, with pale pink flowers. *Geranium sanguineum* is lower-growing and forms a mat of finely cut leaves, ideal for the front of a border. It's a rather loud, bright magenta, while the pure white form, 'Album', is a subtle creature that is best planted in front of more modest growers such as *Rosa* 'Margaret Merril' or among 'Flower Carpet White' on a sunny bank.

Knautia macedonica has small pincushion flowers on slender stems. It's often mistaken for a small, dark red scabious. Growing to 60cm (2ft) or more, it's a light, airy plant and its deep red colouring makes it a

Scarlet Floribunda roses, achilleas and dark red *Knautia macedonica* make a smouldering combination with smoky-bronze fennel and feathery *Stipa gigantea*.

good mixer. The variety 'Melton Pastels' is widely available and includes shades of pink and red. Both this form and the species are good with deep-red English roses such as 'William Shakespeare 2000'.

Penstemons are gems of the summer border. Shrub-like perennials, they're evergreen and form upright bushes that carry short spikes of long, bell-shaped flowers from midsummer through to the onset of winter – sometimes until Christmas. There are many varieties. If you have space to fill, grow *Penstemon* 'Andenken an Friedrich Hahn' (previously known as 'Garnet'). This has narrow leaves and

crimson flowers and grows to 90cm (3ft). It's good with deep-red Floribunda roses such as 'Evelyn Fison' or 'Help for Heroes' and in combination with red foliage shrubs.

Sedum 'Herbstfreude' ('Autumn Joy') is a real stalwart of late summer and autumn. Its upright stems and fleshy, pale green leaves are topped with flattened heads of deep-pink flowers that are much loved by late butterflies. The flower colour deepens to burgundy as the season progresses and the plant becomes lovelier. It's a wonderful planting partner for the large, soft deep-pink and old-gold blooms of the rose 'Jubilee Celebration'.

Sedum 'Herbstfreude', asters and dahlias form a rich and mellow partnership with roses in autumn.

Rich blues and purples

Penstemon 'Raven' is slender with deep-purple flowers. It's stunning in summer combined with pink roses, such as 'Bonica' or 'Ballerina', and glorious with the apricot tints of 'Buff Beauty'. For late blues in the border, look to the salvias. These are spiky bloomers with aromatic foliage and tiny flowers crowded up strong, square stems. The varieties of *Salvia nemorosa* are the shortest. 'Ostfriesland' has violet-purple flowers and tiny purple bracts on 45cm (18in) stems. The bracts persist and add colour after the flowers have faded. It's a good choice in front of lower-growing Hybrid Teas and Floribunda roses. *Salvia × superba* 'Violet Queen' grows to 60cm (2ft), with violet-blue flowers and bracts. It is divine alongside gold roses such as 'Golden Celebration', especially with purple foliage shrubs.

For a later alternative to delphiniums, monkshood (*Aconitum*) is a good choice. This is an upright perennial that needs no support. With finely cut foliage and curious hooded flowers, it rises between the mounds of shrubs and other perennials. *Aconitum* 'Spark's Variety' has branched flower stems reaching 1.5m (5ft) and very deep-blue flowers. Its slender habit means it can rise above larger Shrub roses, such as the pale pink 'Felicia'.

Remember that monkshood is highly poisonous if ingested.

No mixed border is complete without *Verbena bonariensis.* Tall, slender stems carry small heads of tiny, brilliant purple, orange-eyed flowers way above surrounding plants. The flowering season is long, and although the plants don't always overwinter, they generally seed themselves. The colour and character of this perennial make it the perfect partner for the late flowers of roses of all types.

Flowering shrubs

A great number of flowering shrubs can be planted with roses. Many summer-flowering shrubs continue to flower after the roses have bloomed, extending the season of interest while maintaining the character of the planting. Most flowering shrubs are reasonably large, and therefore associate best with Shrub and English roses. However, some of the smaller ones can be grown alongside Modern Bush roses.

Don't forget

Feed your flowering shrubs with rose fertilizer at the same time as you feed your roses. The high potash content in the feed will encourage more flowers and help to ripen growth.

Smaller shrubs

These grow to less than 1m (40in) in height, so are ideal in smaller gardens and combined with Hybrid Teas and compact Floribundas.

Potentillas are easy to grow and have single, buttercup-like flowers. They bloom for a long time (usually from early summer to late autumn) and are attractive to bees and pollinating insects. Some are too harshly coloured to combine with roses, but those in softer shades often work well. Both *Potentilla fruticosa* 'Primrose Beauty', with pale yellow flowers and grey-green foliage, and 'Abbotswood', with white flowers and grey foliage, make good planting partners for roses.

Spiraeas are real survivors, growing on any soil. Probably the most useful with roses is the deep red-pink *Spiraea japonica* 'Anthony Waterer'. This forms a clump of upright stems with flattened heads of flowers from midsummer to late autumn. Team it with the single, pink Rugosa rose 'Fru Dagmar Hastrup' for a tough combination that will grow where many other garden plants fear to tread.

Larger shrubs

These all grow to around 1.5m (5ft) and so are suitable at the back of a border or between Shrub roses. Prune summer-flowering shrubs in midsummer, straight after flowering. Prune later-flowering varieties in late winter. Evergreens can be tidied up in early spring.

The deciduous, pale blue *Ceanothus* × *delileanus* 'Gloire de Versailles' is an excellent plant that is often overlooked. It produces plentiful flowers in early summer and again in autumn, coinciding perfectly with the two main flowering seasons of roses. It has a lovely, graceful habit and looks particularly fine with the single, yellow *Rosa* 'Golden Wings'.

Some of the smaller buddleias make good partners for Shrub roses. *Buddleja* 'Lochinch' is quite large and can reach 2m (6ft), so is a good choice for the back of a border or the centre of a large bed. Its silver-grey foliage combines beautifully with most roses, as do the lavender-blue flowers, which are produced in large sprays and are deliciously scented as well as being magnets for butterflies. The Nanho varieties of buddleia are better for smaller gardens. They rarely reach 1.5m (5ft) and are lighter and twiggier in habit. The richly coloured, fragrant *Buddleja* 'Nanho Purple' mixes with any colour; try it with the fragrant,

The blue-green foliage and red-brown hips of *Rosa glauca* and the single, pink blooms of *Anemone hupehensis* 'Hadspen Abundance' make a lovely planting combination for autumn.

deep-pink *Rosa* 'Wild Edric'. Both plants are tough customers that will survive less than ideal conditions in the garden.

Autumn colour

As autumn advances, the foliage of many deciduous shrubs and perennials develops rich hues of orange, flame and gold. Dark purple berberis leaves glow scarlet, and spiraeas turn from green and gold to flame. Peonies develop rich russet tones, and the sapphire-blue flowers of ceratostigma are displayed against leaves of gold and orange. These autumn hues change the colour balance of the border, and form different relationships with the late blooms of roses. Gold, red and orange roses work in harmony with the hues of autumn leaves, while pink and purple blooms sympathize with blue and purple asters and sugar-pink nerines.

Climbers to grow with Climbing roses

You can make more of your Climbing roses by growing other types of climber through them. This creates exciting combinations of colour and flower form in the height of summer and will also extend the season of interest when the roses aren't flowering. The main point you have to remember is to choose climbers that won't compete with and swamp the roses. Also, select climbers that need pruning at the same time as the rose, otherwise things could get complicated.

Clematis to grow with roses

There are so many advantages to teaming clematis with Climbing roses (*see* box, opposite).

The best clematis to choose are those that flower on the current season's growth, as these bloom in late summer and autumn and are pruned in late winter to early spring, at the same time as roses. These include the mauve-blue *Clematis* 'Prince Charles', which contrasts beautifully with the soft-yellow rose 'The Pilgrim' (*see* right). The clematis has light, fine growth and small, nodding blooms, so it suits the shorter habit of the rose. Another good combination is *Clematis* 'Petit Faucon', which has mauve, yellow-eyed flowers that look magnificent with the pink rose 'Gertrude Jekyll' (*see* right). *Clematis* 'Abundance' has stunning, soft red-purple rounded flowers with creamy-yellow anthers that are accentuated when combined with yellow roses, such as 'Lady Hillingdon' (*see* below right). Other later-flowering clematis that look good with roses include 'Étoile Violette', 'Perle d'Azur', 'Niobe' and 'Polish Spirit'.

Some large-flowering clematis flower in late spring and early summer, on wood produced the previous year. These can be grown through roses, but you'll need to prune them after their first flowers have faded. As these tend to be light growers with upright stems, this isn't too difficult and usually means you're pruning the clematis when dead-heading the rose. Popular varieties include 'Nelly Moser', 'Miss Bateman' and 'Lasurstern'.

Some gardeners recommend early-flowering clematis, such as *Clematis alpina*, *Clematis macropetala* and *Clematis montana*, to add interest before the rose comes into bloom. However, although this is a good idea in theory, it attracts attention to the rose when it's not looking its best. Also, early-flowering clematis aren't pruned at the same time as roses, which makes management tricky. *Clematis montana* is far too vigorous for most Climbing roses anyway.

Clematis 'Prince Charles'

Rosa 'The Pilgrim'

Rosa 'Gertrude Jekyll'

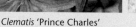

Clematis 'Petit Faucon'

Rosa 'Lady Hillingdon'

Clematis 'Abundance'

Why roses and clematis make good companions

■ Clematis have light stems and cling gently to a support by twining their leaf-stalks around another stem or wire, or whatever they can hang onto. Therefore, they will not strangle a rose they're growing through.

■ Clematis offer a different colour range from roses, as they're rich in blues and purples and therefore complement the colour palette of the rose. There are few yellow clematis, while roses excel in this part of the spectrum.

■ Most Climbing roses are fragrant and most clematis are not, so the roses make up for the clematis.

■ Climbing roses and clematis like similar growing conditions: both require a rich, fertile soil and plenty of water during the growing season.

■ Clematis and roses both benefit from fertilizers high in nitrogen and potash.

■ As they both suffer from the same or similar pests and diseases, clematis and roses require the same treatments in the form of insecticides and fungicides.

Annual climbers to grow with roses

Annual climbers are a great way of adding another flower form and colour to a Climbing rose. They also extend the season by continuing to bloom throughout late summer and into autumn. Ongoing maintenance is easy – after the annuals have grown and bloomed, you just strip away the faded stems in winter and replant with new annuals the following year. There's no need to prune or worry that they'll swamp your precious roses in years to come.

Here are some recommended annual climbers to go with roses:

Cobaea scandens with repeat-flowering Climbing roses
Ipomoea tricolor 'Heavenly Blue' with white Climbing roses
Thunbergia alata with orange or copper Climbing roses

Don't forget

Both clematis and roses like a bit of personal space. Make sure you plant the clematis at least 60cm (2ft) away from the rose, otherwise it will struggle to establish and will provide competition for the rose.

Other climbers to grow with roses

Although clematis is the most common climber to grow with roses, there are plenty of other options. The pink-and-white splashed leaves of *Actinidia kolomikta* make a glorious backdrop for the double-flowered pink Shrub rose 'Bonica', and the lantern-like, rich red, purple or pink flowers of *Rhodochiton atrosanguineus* look stunning combined with pink roses such as 'New Dawn' (*see right*). The rhodochiton flowers well into autumn, so helps to continue the display when the rose starts to run out of steam.

The other climbing plant that springs to mind when we think of roses is honeysuckle (*Lonicera*), with its delicate flowers and sweet scent. Honeysuckles are woodland plants by origin, so they're a good choice for partial shade. As they mature, they twine their stems around a support, so when growing them with a rose you'll need to choose a vigorous rose variety and be prepared to sort the honeysuckle out by hard pruning periodically. The best variety to grow is *Lonicera periclymenum* 'Graham Thomas', which has pale creamy-yellow flowers over a long period. It's not as vigorous as many honeysuckles, so is therefore less threatening to the rose. An ideal planting partner would be *Rosa* 'Golden Gate'. Other honeysuckles that combine well with roses include *Lonicera periclymenum* 'Belgica', the early Dutch honeysuckle, which flowers from late spring to early summer, and 'Serotina', the late Dutch honeysuckle, which blooms from midsummer to autumn.

If you have a warm, sheltered garden, you could try growing roses with *Jasminum polyanthum*. This has dark green leaves, slender twining stems and deliciously

Actinidia kolomikta

Rosa 'Bonica'

Rhodochiton atrosanguineus   Rosa 'New Dawn'

fragrant white flowers in very early summer with the first of the roses. Avoid the hardy jasmine (*Jasminum officinale*) as it forms such a dense tangle of stems it will quickly smother the rose.

Planting and growing

Roses aren't difficult to grow, but they need some attention if you're to get the best from them. At the planting stage, do everything you can to give them the best possible start: improve the soil if necessary, and plant them properly to ensure their establishment and success. Once they begin to grow, remember to feed them, keep a vigilant eye open for pests and diseases that can spoil your efforts, and give them a helping hand by pruning and training.

Buying roses

Going back a few years, you would have bought all your roses in late autumn, winter or early spring as dormant, bare-root plants, dug up from the field. Their roots might have been wrapped, with a little peat around them, and the plant may have been boxed, bagged or wrapped in straw. Today, roses are still available bare-root, but more often than not they're sold in containers in garden centres and can be purchased and planted at pretty much any time of year.

Always buy roses from a reputable nursery or garden centre to ensure you get a healthy specimen and the correct variety.

What to look for

The first step to growing roses successfully is to choose good, healthy plants in the first place. It's not worth buying poor-quality specimens, even if they are cheaper. Never make your choice based entirely on how many buds and flowers a plant has. Instead, look for the following features, which are a better indication of all-round health.

■ An evenly branched plant, with at least three main stems well spaced on all sides of the plant. Avoid one-sided plants with fewer than three strong stems.
■ Sturdy, undamaged stems, with no crossing branches.
■ Buds that are plump, and not shrivelled and wrinkled.
■ A well-developed, healthy root system that is larger than the top of the plant (if dormant), assuming the stems have been cut back to 15–30cm (6–12in).
■ If buying containerized roses, choose plants that look as if they have been freshly potted. Avoid those with moss or weeds on the top of the compost, as they're likely to be last season's stock, which never performs as well.
■ In the growing season, look for strong, healthy foliage with no signs of disease.

Bare-root roses

You're most likely to buy bare-root roses from a specialist nursery, direct or by mail order. If you can't plant them straight away, heel them in somewhere in your garden until you're ready to plant them (*see* below right). This basically means covering the roots with soil or compost until you're ready to plant. Alternatively, put them in a large pot or bucket and cover the roots with moist compost. Don't be tempted to keep bare-root roses in the house or in the greenhouse before planting; this may coax them into growth, which will be hit by frost when you plant them out.

Containerized roses

A rose sold in a container will have been grown in the ground and lifted during autumn, when it would have been potted in suitable compost containing slow-release nutrients. It may be sold in autumn, or the following spring or summer, when its roots will be more established. The advantage of buying a containerized rose is that there is no hurry to plant it. Also, if you buy roses in summer you can see what the flowers look like in reality and, just as importantly, it gives you the opportunity to smell them.

Heeling in

Ideally, plant your bare-root roses as soon as you get them. However, if this isn't possible you'll need to 'heel' them in until you're ready to plant. In a sheltered area of the garden, dig a small trench and lay the rose in it. Cover the roots and graft union with soil, gently firm in and water well. Keep the soil moist.

Growing conditions

Roses aren't difficult plants to grow, but like many other garden plants they have their likes and dislikes. To get the best from your roses you need to pay attention to their growing conditions. This may also influence your choice of varieties, since different types of rose are adapted to different types of soil, aspect and climate. Most roses respond to a little pampering, and rose lovers will not begrudge them some special attention.

Aspect

Nearly all roses need a minimum of four hours direct sunshine a day during the growing season to thrive. Some varieties are better suited to shady sites than others and these are the ones to go for if the planting site is shaded by the house, surrounding walls or fences, or neighbouring trees (*see* pages 120–21). Beware of planting a tall, dense shrub to the side of a rose where the sun comes

from. This could put the rose in the shade and rob it of those valuable hours of direct sunlight. Also, avoid planting a bushy rose under the overhanging branches of a tree. As well as not liking the shade, the rose will dislike the competition with the tree roots for water and nutrients. Rambler roses, however, are happy in this situation, as they're naturally adapted to scramble up through the branches of trees to reach the light.

Generally, roses do well in an open situation with plenty of air circulation around the plants, which helps to prevent disease. However, avoid very exposed, windy situations if possible (*see* page 122).

Soil

Roses have strong, woody roots with few fibrous side roots, so they do best in a firm soil that provides good anchorage rather than an open, loose soil that gives little stability to the plants. They also prefer a rich but free-draining soil. If you don't have the ideal soil you can nearly always improve it so that roses will thrive, particularly if you choose more robust varieties, such as any of the Gallica or Rugosa Shrub roses, or certain Floribundas or English roses.

Weeding and mulching

Roses are much happier and healthier without competition from weeds. Check regularly for annual weeds and remove them by hand, or by gently hoeing around the plants, taking care not to damage roots and the base of the stems. If stubborn perennial weeds, such as bindweed or ground elder, become a problem, they can be carefully treated with a systemic herbicide containing glyphosate, but you must take great care not to get the chemical on the rose stems or leaves. Never spray in hot weather, as the chemical can vaporize and harm the rose foliage.

Mulching around the plants with chipped bark, good garden compost, composted bracken or composted straw helps to suppress weeds and prevent annual ones from germinating. It also keeps the soil cool in summer and conserves moisture. Always apply a mulch when the soil is moist.

Add organic matter, such as manure or garden compost, to the soil before planting to give your roses a great start.

Your garden soil

When growing roses in the garden, it's vital to know what soil type you have, as its make-up will have a bearing on how well your roses will grow and which types you should plant. All soil types benefit from the addition of organic matter, such as good garden compost, well-rotted manure or spent mushroom compost. It improves the quality, texture and fertility of garden soil, helps dry soils to hold moisture and nutrients and encourages worms, which are valuable for aerating heavy soil. Add organic matter when planting new roses, as a feed for established ones and as a mulch spread around the base of your roses. Although roses prefer a slightly acid soil, as long as you feed regularly with a rose fertilizer, and mulch with well-rotted manure or compost, your roses should be fine whatever your soil pH.

SOIL TYPE			ADVANTAGES	DISADVANTAGES	HOW TO IMPROVE THE SOIL
Loam		Soft and can be squeezed into a ball but is easily rubbed into crumbs again	Loam, especially medium loam, is ideal for roses – it drains quickly, holds on to moisture and nutrients and is easy to work throughout the year	None	Although less essential than with other soil types, add well-rotted manure and garden compost to boost levels of organic matter
Clay soil		Forms sticky, heavy clumps when wet and is hard and solid when dry	Moist, fertile and firm so provides nutrients and good anchorage for roses	Heavy and dense, so digging is usually hard work	Add bulky organic matter, such as garden compost or manure, to improve its texture and make digging easier
Sandy soil		Feels gritty, dry and loose-textured	Light and therefore easy for the gardener to work	Often lacks sufficient fertility and moisture for roses to do well	Add garden compost or manure every couple of years to give the soil body and increase its water- and nutrient-holding capacity. Feed twice a year with a good-quality rose food
Chalky soil		Loose texture and usually full of lumps of chalk	Roses are happy in chalk, provided there is sufficient soil depth above the chalk, 40cm (16in) or so	Chalky soils are often dry and shallow, so do not provide sufficient moisture or support for roses	Add plenty of compost or manure on a regular basis to help the soil to hold on to water and nutrients
Peaty soil		Dark, open-textured and can be rather crumbly	None	Moist, acidic and low in fertility – the most difficult soil for growing roses	Add good loamy topsoil in the area where you intend to plant your roses, as well as organic matter after planting

Planting roses

So, you've chosen your roses, decided where you're going to plant them and what they're going to look good with, and have improved the soil if necessary with plenty of organic matter. Now it's a question of planting your new roses properly to get them off to the best possible start – good planting techniques mean healthy roses.

If we want roses to become fully established in the garden, we need to make it attractive to them. Make sure the planting hole is large enough to take the roots without being crammed in – all too often, the establishment of new plants is hindered by a hole that is barely larger than the roots. Also, ensure the soil around roses is well cultivated rather than compacted, otherwise the new roots won't want to venture forth into such an inhospitable environment. Fork over the planting site thoroughly, adding plenty of good garden compost or well-rotted manure and mycorrhizal fungal granules (*see* box, page 50). Once you've planted the rose, firm it in well and add plenty of water.

(*see* box, page 50)

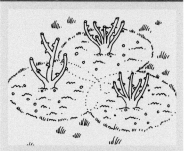

Planting in threes

Where space permits, it's a good idea to plant Modern Bush roses and smaller Shrub and English roses in threes, about 60–80cm (24–32in) apart. The three roses will grow together to make one larger shrub. Planted in this way, the roses will make a greater impact in the border and will be easier to feed and prune. It also means that the space is kept for the roses, rather than being occupied by other plants that would compete for moisture and nutrients.

Don't forget

The compost may fall away from the roots of recently potted roses when you remove them from their containers. This usually happens in autumn and should not affect their establishment. Just carry on and plant them, keeping as much compost as possible around the roots.

Containerized roses can be planted at any time of year, while bare-root specimens can be planted only when dormant, between late autumn and mid-spring.

Planting depth of roses

It's vital to plant the rose at the correct depth, and to make sure the roots have plenty of space to spread out. Placing a cane across the hole makes it easier to judge the depth is correct. The graft union, which is the swollen area between the roots and the branches, should always be slightly below soil level.

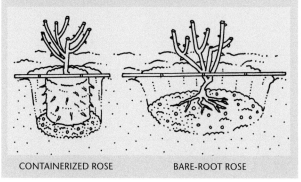

CONTAINERIZED ROSE   BARE-ROOT ROSE

Planting bare-root and containerized roses

You can plant a bare-root rose any time you like between late autumn and mid-spring, providing the soil isn't frozen. Ideally, plant the rose as soon as you get it. If the roots are dry, perhaps because the rose has just arrived by post, soak them for an hour or two in a bucket of water. If you can't plant a bare-root rose straightaway, heel it into the soil (*see* box, page 45) before planting it in its final position (*see* right).

Containerized roses can be planted at any time of the year, providing the soil isn't frozen and is adequately moist. Before planting, thoroughly soak the compost and allow it to drain. If planting in summer, it may be best to immerse the container in a bucket of water for at least ten minutes to make sure the compost has been saturated.

To plant a containerized rose, dig a large hole, approximately 60cm (2ft) across and deeper than the container. Prepare the planting hole as for bare-root roses, slide the plant very carefully out of its pot to avoid harming the young, fibrous roots, and plant the rose in the centre of the hole, checking you have the rose at the correct depth (*see* opposite). You may need to tease out the roots at the base of the rootball to encourage them to grow out into the soil. Backfill with garden soil mixed with compost and fertilizer, firm and water thoroughly.

Don't forget

If you have a relatively shallow soil, choose shorter roses; taller varieties may topple over if the soil depth is insufficient.

HOW TO plant a bare-root rose

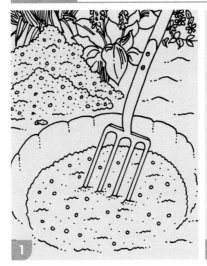

1 Dig a hole that is wide enough to hold the rose's roots when spread out. Long roots can be snipped back to about 20cm (8in). The hole should be deep enough for the bud union to sit just below soil level when planted. Break up the soil in the base of the hole with a fork.

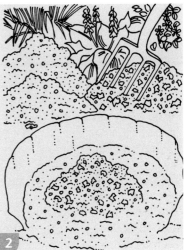

2 Mix the soil removed from the hole with garden compost, well-rotted manure or shrub-planting compost and place a little of this at the bottom of the planting hole. Sprinkle a handful of rose fertilizer over the top. Add another handful of fertilizer to the remaining soil and compost mixture.

3 Position the rose in the centre of the hole and spread out the roots. Backfill the hole with the soil and compost mixture; check the planting depth, as shown opposite. It's a good idea to leave the soil a little indented around the base of the rose so as to direct rainfall into the rootball.

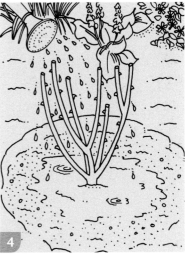

4 Firm the soil with your feet to ensure the rose is secure in the soil. This is important, as wind and bad weather can easily rock the plant, dislodging its roots and preventing establishment. Water the plant thoroughly after planting, and then regularly once growth starts in spring.

A dark blue wall provides the ideal backdrop for the exquisite, delicate-looking flowers of 'Cécile Brünner'. This rose tolerates partial shade, but blooms only once, in midsummer.

Planting Climbing and Rambler roses

When planting a Climbing or Rambler rose, the distance of the rose to its support is a key consideration. The rose needs to be close enough to reach its support easily, but not so close that the soil is poor, as is often the case at the base of a wall or fence. You should also consider whether you'll need to maintain the wall or fence during the lifetime of the rose.

Plant the rose at a distance of at least 60cm (2ft) from the wall or fence and lean the stems towards the support, leaving the canes in place. Dig as large a hole as possible, add plenty of organic matter and sprinkle a handful of rose fertilizer in the bottom of the planting hole to help the rose to get going. Encourage the rose to climb towards its support and keep the rose regularly watered until it's established.

When planting a Rambler to grow up a tree, do not attempt to plant it right up against the trunk, but 80–100cm (32–40in) away, between the trunk and drip line of the tree. The drip line is where the branches extend to above ground, and usually where the roots extend to below. The edge of the root system is the most active here, so this is where the tree roots give most competition. (For supporting Climbing and Rambler roses, *see* pages 52–6).

How to plant a Climbing rose against a wall

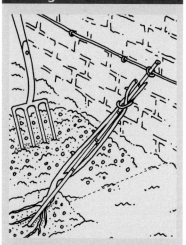

Dig a planting hole at least 60cm (2ft) away from the wall or fence. Prepare the ground thoroughly, and plant as you would any other rose (*see* page 49), but with the roots sloping away from the wall. Angle the stems towards their support and tie in if necessary.

How to avoid rose replant sickness

It can be difficult establishing a rose where another one has died or been removed. Sometimes a problem known as rose replant sickness can occur (*see also* page 74).

Gardeners used to recommend that if you wanted to replace a rose you should remove a cubic yard of soil from the original planting site and add the same amount of good loam before planting a new specimen. The amount of effort this entailed meant it was often better to think again and plant something else.

Today, experts believe that rose replant sickness can be avoided simply by adding mycorrhizal fungal granules at the time of planting. Trials have shown that rose roots form a symbiotic association with microscopic fungi in garden soil, making it easier for the rose to absorb water and nutrients, thus promoting more vigorous growth. When a rose dies or is removed, these microscopic fungi in the soil die away, and it's difficult for a new rose to establish a new association.

The granules – which can be sprinkled into the base of the planting hole before planting a containerized rose, or over the moist roots of a bare-root rose – will help the new specimen to establish itself and flourish. The preparation seems to work and is well worth the additional investment when planting any rose, whether or not you're replacing an existing one.

Don't forget

Although roses associate happily with other shrubs and perennials, they dislike stiff competition from their neighbours. Give each plant enough space to develop and reach its potential. If roses are overpowered by their neighbours, growth will be weak and drawn and they will be more susceptible to disease. (See pages 26–43 for suitable planting companions in mixed borders.)

Feeding and watering

Roses are greedy feeders; they like plenty of nutrients in the soil, and on most soils manure or garden compost is simply not enough. If your roses lack one or more of the key nutrients, you'll find growth is weak, the leaves may be small, pale or discoloured, flowering may be poor and the rose will be more susceptible to pests and diseases, such as black spot and rust. To get the most out of your roses, you'll need to feed them.

Tomato fertilizer applied during the growing season will encourage your roses to flower more freely.

Using fertilizers and liquid feeds

Powder or granular rose fertilizers contain all the three major plant nutrients (*see* chart, below), plus other beneficial nutrients and trace elements, such as magnesium and iron, in smaller quantities. You need to apply rose fertilizer generously twice a year – in early spring just as growth is starting, and again in midsummer after that first flush of flowers. This second feed is particularly important to ensure repeat flowering, to strengthen the plants and help prevent disease. To apply rose fertilizer, sprinkle the granules or powder over the surface of the ground around the rose, ideally within 60cm (2ft) of the centre of the plant. Use the amount recommended by the manufacturer, but bear in mind you'll need slightly more for a large Shrub rose than for a small Modern Bush rose. Stir it into the soil surface with a hoe or long-handled weed fork and water thoroughly if the weather is dry.

Blood, fish and bone is an alternative slow-release feed for roses. Use it in the same way as you would the general granular feed. The advantage is that it is organic. However, it usually contains only the main nutrients, plus a little iron, and does not include other beneficial nutrients or trace elements.

Liquid feeds, which you dilute in a watering can, are useful as an additional boost during the growing season. Tomato fertilizer is probably the best choice, because it has a high potash content which the roses will appreciate. However, it is a short-term tonic only, as it is quickly absorbed by the plants or washed from the soil.

Avoid using growmore on roses. Roses prefer a slower-release fertilizer; also, it lacks the iron and magnesium that roses need.

Watering

Once established, roses will tolerate dry conditions, but they grow better, bloom more and are less susceptible to disease when there is adequate moisture in the soil. Watering is particularly important after feeding, as it makes the nutrients accessible to the roses. Water regularly in dry weather, around the base of the plants, not over the flowers and foliage. A soft spray or a gradual trickle is more effective than a fierce deluge from a jet spray or high-pressure hose.

Don't forget

Don't allow granular fertilizer to come into contact with the plant and always stick to the amount recommended by the manufacturer; otherwise it can do more harm than good.

The main nutrients roses need

The chart below shows the main plant nutrients needed by roses. Roses also require other nutrients and trace elements in smaller amounts. These are the vitamins and minerals of the plant food world that help to keep them healthy. Iron and magnesium are especially important for the healthy growth of garden hybrid roses.

PLANT FOOD	WHAT IT'S FOR
Nitrogen (N)	Stimulates the growth of stems and leaves
Phosphorus/phosphate (P)	Encourages root development in newly planted roses. It is also beneficial to established roses, although they need less of it than nitrogen and potassium
Potassium/potash (K)	Promotes bud and flower development and helps to harden soft growth, making foliage firm and more resistant to weather and disease

Supporting roses

Most Modern Bush roses need no additional support; they're sturdy enough to stay upright by themselves. However, some Shrub roses, including the taller English roses, have a rather lax habit. Their stems may be upright at the beginning of the season but later flop under the weight of foliage and flowers, spoiling the effect, so these need staking for best results. Climbing and Rambler roses also need support in the form of walls, fences, trees and decorative garden structures such as pergolas and arches. (*See also* pages 114–18.)

Staking Shrub roses

If your main aim is to keep a Shrub rose in shape and show off its flowers to best effect, you'll need to provide a support that is as unobtrusive as possible. However, bear in mind that it needs to be strong enough to support the weight of the rose in full growth. The secret of success when staking a Shrub rose is to put the stake in place at the beginning of the season, before growth gets going, rather than wrestling with it when the rose is in flower. The most effective method is to create a kind of cage to support the rose (*see* box, right).

Lighter, smaller Shrub roses can benefit from herbaceous plant supports, available from garden centres. These are basically half-hoops on two legs. The hoops support the rose stems and prevent them from drooping.

Decorative structures

Structures like arches, pergolas and obelisks are ideal for supporting roses and make delightful features in the garden (*see* pages 114–18). They add essential height, create a focal point, provide an entrance to a different part of the garden, and offer an invitation to explore further.

(See also pages 114–18.)

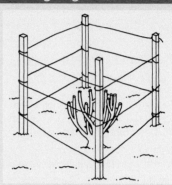

After planting, drive three or four stout wooden posts into the ground, about 50cm (20in) from the centre of the rose. The stakes should be approximately 1.5m (5ft) long and 4cm (1¾in) across and dug to 30–50cm (12–20in) deep. Wind flexible plastic tie or strong twine between the posts, spiralling it around the structure and wrapping it around the posts to create a 'cage'.

When the rose has put on growth and is in flower, the supports should be mostly hidden and the crown of the plant will be above the posts and tie, giving a naturally arching effect.

They also give you a chance to grow roses that you might not otherwise have room for. For a display closer to the ground, you can train roses over willow or hazel hoops pushed into the ground (*see* box, page 30). It's vital you match the rose to the structure; many can be too vigorous for smaller structures and you don't

Don't forget

Make sure that decorative structures are well anchored and that they will stand up under the considerable weight of the roses in full flower.

Training a rose to grow horizontally on a support will encourage the growth of more flowering sideshoots.

want to keep chopping the rose back. Also, remember that roses make a stunning display if combined with other climbers, such as clematis or honeysuckle (*see* pages 42–3).

Obelisks

Usually made of metal or wood, an obelisk can be a highly decorative feature in the garden, even in winter and without the addition of a rose. Ornamental obelisks suit formal garden designs, particularly where they're used as focal points in beds of short Modern Bush roses. If you decide to grow a rose up an obelisk, you must choose a structure that is tall enough and strong enough to take the weight – 2m (6ft) high is really a minimum, with a spread of at least 60cm (2ft) at the base. Choose roses with light stems and a trailing habit (*see* pages 115–16).

Training around the structure can be more difficult if the obelisk is angular in design. You may need to train the main stems up the uprights to start with, then take out the growing-tips to encourage sideshoots, which can be tied in periodically. Do this at intervals until the plant reaches the top.

Rustic tripods

Rustic timber tripods are well suited to the heavy stems of roses, and this is a good way to support tall, vigorous Shrub roses and some Climbing roses (*see* pages 115–16).

Don't forget

Obelisks made of light willow and cane can be very effective, and are lovely for sweet peas and delicate, light-stemmed climbers, but they are not nearly robust enough for roses.

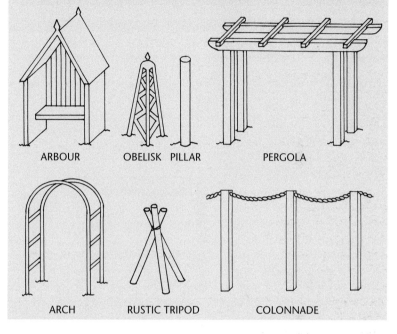

Decorative supports

There are many different types of support for roses, and they are available in a wide range of sizes and styles. Many are easy to make yourself using basic tools and equipment.

ARBOUR   OBELISK PILLAR   PERGOLA

ARCH   RUSTIC TRIPOD   COLONNADE

This type of structure suits a less formal garden and can be used in a mixed border, to screen an eyesore or even in the corner of a paddock.

To make a rustic tripod, you just need three strong, round stakes, at least 3m (10ft) in length and 10cm (4in) in diameter. Drive them into the ground at an angle so that they're at least 1m (40in) apart at the base. Tie them together at the top using rope or heavy galvanized wire. Plant the rose in the middle and encourage it to drape its stems across the supports as it grows. Tie stems in place as necessary.

Arches

An archway to support roses can be made from metal or wood. There are various lightweight arches made

from heavy-gauge, plastic-coated wire that are available in kit form. Before you select one of these, make sure that it's robust enough to support roses. If you like the idea of a metal-framed arch, you may be better opting for a heavier structure that comes in two halves that bolt together. The base of these is usually best concreted into the ground for extra stability.

You can buy a ready-made heavy timber arch, or you can make your own with four posts and some

Don't forget

When working out the height of your arch or pergola, remember that fully grown roses can occupy up to 30cm (12in) of space below the top of the structure. Make sure you allow enough headroom to walk underneath.

If you let a rose grow vertically only, for instance straight up a post or pillar, all the flowers appear at the top of the stems, where you won't be able to see them. To ensure roses flower all the way up, and to provide interest at eye level, train them spirally as they grow.

timber or heavy trellis to put across the top and up the sides. Just remember that once the rose has grown over the arch it will be virtually impossible to maintain or repair the structure, so make it strong and simple.

When choosing a rose for an arch (*see* pages 114–15), you want one with pliable stems that will bend around the supports and elegantly over the top. It's best to avoid very vigorous and upright varieties.

Don't forget

If you're making decorative supports out of untreated wood, use a plant-friendly wood preservative, applying two coats to the part that will be buried in the ground; you don't want the wood to rot and have the structure fall over when your rose has grown up it. Allow the preservative to dry thoroughly before you put the post in the ground.

Supporting roses on trees

Vigorous Rambler roses have large, downward-pointing thorns that act as grappling hooks to help them cling on as they climb. To get them going, it may be necessary to tie the stems into the trunk of the tree using flexible plastic ties until they reach branches they can cling onto. Remember, a rampant Rambler growing through the branches of a tree adds a lot of stems and foliage. This will increase the wind resistance of the tree, which could be a problem if the tree is old, weak or in an exposed situation. The rose will also compete with the tree both in the soil and in the air. If the rose is a vigorous variety, it will win in the long run. For suggestions of roses suitable for growing through trees, *see* page 118.

Arbours

An arbour fitted with a seat is the best way to create the feeling of an arch if you don't have a sensible location for a freestanding arch. It can be positioned against a wall or fence at the side of the garden, where it will make an attractive focal point and destination in the garden picture, as well as providing a sheltered, secluded seating area. Any of the roses suitable for an archway can be draped over it (*see* pages 114–15), perhaps combined with fragrant honeysuckle or jasmine. Some arbours are backed with trellis, so you could grow another kind of climber behind the seat.

Pergolas

A pergola is really a series of archways positioned to make a tunnel (*see* pages 114–15). Pergolas need robust, solid uprights, not only for support but also for appearance; a pergola with spindly legs simply does not look right. The great thing about a pergola is that because you need the roses to grow up and over

---

HOW TO train a rose up a vertical support

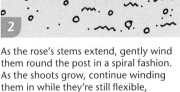

1. Plant a Climbing or Rambler rose 40–60cm (16–24in) away from its support. Position the rose so that the main stem leans into the post, then tie in the stems using flexible plastic tie.

2. As the rose's stems extend, gently wind them round the post in a spiral fashion. As the shoots grow, continue winding them in while they're still flexible, keeping them fairly close together.

the top of the structure to cover it, you can use some of the more vigorous varieties of Climbing and Rambler roses. The bigger the pergola, the more vigorous the roses you will be able to accommodate.

Pillars and colonnades

Short Climbing roses and some of the more slender Shrub roses can be grown on pillars (*see* pages 115–16). These are straightforward poles, usually pushed into the back of a border. All you have to do is drive a strong round post into the soil and plant the rose alongside it. Position the rose so that the stems lean into the post. You'll need a post that is at least 2.5m (8ft) in length, allowing for 60cm (2ft) below ground. As the rose grows, train the shoots around the stem in a spiral to encourage sideshoots and flowers from the bottom of the post to the top (*see* opposite). If you train the shoots straight up the post, you may have flowers at the top and nothing at the bottom. Cut off the top of the rose flush with the top of the post each year in winter.

You can create a much grander effect by growing Climbing or Rambler roses up heavy posts linked by thick swags of rope. This is known as a colonnade, and can be spectacular at the back of a border or across a garden to divide areas (*see* right and page 115).

Don't forget

If you're creating a colonnade, it's best to choose one variety of rose, or two and alternate them along the colonnade, rather than having lots of different types which can look messy.

HOW TO create a colonnade

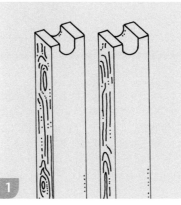

1 Using a small bow saw, make notches in the top of all the posts that will make up the supports of the colonnade. The posts need to be really robust, a minimum of 15 x 15cm (6 x 6in) thick, and treated with a preservative. The notches should be around 4cm (1¾in) across and deep, just large enough to hold the rope snugly when it is fitted into them. It's best to buy your rope before you cut the notches to ensure a good fit.

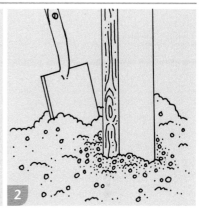

2 Dig a hole about 45cm (18in) across and at least 60cm (2ft) deep for each post and lay half a concrete block at the bottom of each hole to spread the weight. Stand each post upright on its block and fill the hole with concrete, making sure the posts are perfectly perpendicular by using a spirit level. Leave a day or two for the concrete to set completely. Plant the rose alongside the support and tie in the stems as they grow (*see* opposite).

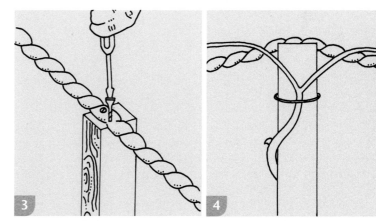

3 Lay strong but decorative rope along the top of the posts and push it down into the notches, then screw it in place. Natural jute rope looks most attractive, and the rose thorns tend to cling onto it more effectively than they do with polypropylene rope. It's important that the rope is fixed securely. The rope can be draped between the posts to create a gentle swag; make sure you allow for shrinkage in rain!

4 When the rose stems reach the top of the post, let them run along the horizontal ropes, tying them in as needed. Prune exactly as for a normal Climbing rose, training the main stem along the rope and shortening the lateral shoots in winter or early spring to three or four buds. When growing a Rambler rose, cut out some of the flowered stems as the blooms fade and tie in new vigorous shoots to progress along the ropes and bloom next season.

Tie in the long stems of Climbing and Rambler roses, bending the shoots over so they grow horizontally.

Plant ties for roses

Many different types of plant tie are available, but not all are suitable for roses. Avoid twist ties: they tend to either fall apart or damage the stems. Strong garden twine is suitable, but it can be quite fiddly to use, especially if you're no good at tying knots. Ideally, choose flexible plastic tie or wire covered with a soft plastic foam coating, because this stretches as the rose stems expand.

Supporting roses against a wall or fence

Trellis is the ideal support for plants that climb using tendrils, twining stems and leaf-stalks. However, it's not the best support for roses, which use thorny stems to hook themselves onto their supports. Although some of the less vigorous, upright Climbing roses can be successfully trained against a heavy trellis panel, strong galvanized wires attached to the wall with vine-eyes make a much better and more versatile support for Climbing and Rambler roses (see right).

As soon as shoots are long enough, they should be tied into the wires, in most cases training them horizontally along the way. The rose naturally wants to grow upwards and flower at the ends of the stems, so you need to take control and bend those shoots over. By doing this you encourage the sideshoots to develop all along the stems. These will produce flowers, so the more sideshoots you encourage, the more flowers you'll be able to enjoy. If you

HOW TO train a rose against a wall

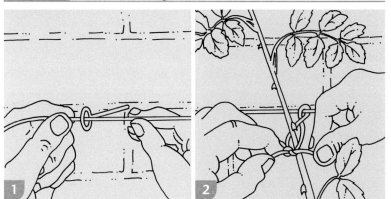

1 Drill holes into the mortar between the bricks for the vine-eyes, setting them at 1m (40in) intervals along the wall and spacing the rows approximately 40–45cm (16–18in) apart. Push a wall plug firmly into each hole, then screw in the vine-eyes. Thread strong wire through the holes; it should be at least 8cm (3in) from the wall. Bend the wire round the final 'eye' to secure it.

2 As the rose grows, tie the rose stems to the wire at regular intervals. Make sure that the stems are not pinned too tightly to the wall, as good air circulation is vital for the health of the rose, preventing diseases such as mildew and black spot. Also, take care not to damage the stems when tying them into the wire. Remember, the rose stems will expand in girth as they grow in length (see box, above).

tie the shoots in regularly during the growing season, you'll also encourage new, vigorous shoots to arise from the base of the plant. For Climbing roses with a very tall, upright habit, such as 'Madame Alfred Carrière', install horizontal wires as you would for other roses, but instead of training the stems horizontally tie them in as they cross the wires, splaying the stems in a fan formation.

Pruning roses

Rose pruning has always been one of the great gardening rituals. Traditionalists take great pride in the task, believing that certain procedures carried out at specific times of year are essential for a rose's success. However, some modern gardeners take a more relaxed approach, claiming that it's no longer necessary to observe such rigid rules. There's no doubt that if you want the best possible display it's well worth understanding the basics of rose pruning, and if done properly it will reward with tidier, healthier plants with more flowers.

Use a pruning saw for thick stems, and remember to wear a thick pair of gloves when pruning roses.

Pruning tools

You'll need a few tools for rose pruning. Treat yourself to good-quality equipment, and if you look after it properly it will last a lifetime.

Secateurs The most essential piece of kit is a pair of secateurs, or pruners; you need ones with sharp blades, and preferably the bypass type. These are the ones with scissor-action blades, rather than anvil secateurs, where one straight sharp blade cuts against another broader, fatter blade. If the latter are not in peak condition, they tend to crush and damage stems.

Loppers If you have large, established roses, particularly Shrub and Climbing roses, you'll also find a strong pair of loppers indispensable. These enable you to reach down into the plants and cut out unwanted stems without getting yourself torn to shreds. Again, bypass loppers are the most desirable, although large anvil loppers may be easier to use on thick, woody stems.

Pruning saw For roses with thick stems, more than about 2.5cm (1in) thick, a pruning saw is useful.

Gloves A good pair of strong, thorn-proof gardening gloves is vital for rose pruning. The gauntlet-type gloves, with a wide cuff that protects your wrist, are best.

Where and how to cut

When pruning, it's important to cut the stem correctly and in the right place. Make a diagonal cut just above a leaf-joint. The cut should slope down behind the node. If you cut too far above it, you'll leave a piece of stem that cannot grow further, so it will die back to the growth bud below. This is known as a snag, and as well as being unsightly, it can be a point where fungal or bacterial infection enters the plant. Leaving snags is not good practice, so make sure you cut about 6mm (¼in) above the bud.

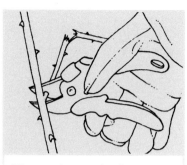

When pruning roses in winter, start by cutting out what are known as the four Ds: dead, damaged, diseased and dying wood. Use secateurs for stems less than 1cm (½in) thick.

Why and when to prune

There are several reasons for pruning roses, or any flowering shrubs for that matter: to control the size, shape and habit of the plants; to remove dead, diseased, damaged and dying wood; to promote growth and the production of flowering shoots; and to remove faded flowers and allow others to develop.

The time to prune depends on the type of rose, the effect you want to achieve and when you plant. Roses planted during the dormant season are pruned on planting, if necessary; containerized roses planted in the growing season should simply be dead-headed after flowering, as for established roses.

Winter pruning

It used to be considered best to prune most roses in mid- to late spring, after the worst of the weather. However, because winters are warmer, and growth usually starts much earlier, it's now considered more appropriate to prune them in late winter to early spring. Pruning in winter avoids cutting off any early new growth, which would waste energy and delay flower development by several weeks. In mild areas late winter is ideal, although you should avoid bouts of really frosty weather. In cold, exposed conditions wait until early spring. The pruning method depends on the type of rose.

Summer pruning

Once your roses have finished flowering in summer, it's a good idea to dead-head them, in other words remove the faded flowers,

Dealing with suckers

Most modern roses have been grafted onto the rootstock of a species rose (*see* page 68). While this is generally beneficial for the rose, the species will attempt to reassert itself by sending out its own shoots, known as suckers, at the base of the plant; if left, the more vigorous species rose will eventually replace the grafted cultivar. To prevent this, you need to remove suckers as soon as they appear – trace them to their point of origin below the soil surface, and pull them away from the parent plant. If you cut them off, some dormant buds are more likely to remain at the base of the shoot to produce more suckers.

Remove the first blooms as they fade to keep the plants looking good and encourage other buds to open. When most blooms have faded, it's worth sacrificing the last few buds to encourage new flowers to form.

to promote the production of more blooms. This applies to all roses except those that will produce attractive hips later in the season (because if you remove the flowers you won't get any hips) and rampant Climbing or Rambler roses, which would be difficult to reach.

To dead-head, when the first few blooms fade, pick or snip these off the stem to leave adjacent buds to develop and take over the display. Once most of the flowers have faded on a stem, cut back to two or three buds behind the cluster. Usually, you'll see another shoot already starting to develop – if so, cut back to just above it. If the rose is a repeat-flowering variety, this will grow to produce further blooms.

Don't forget

Hard pruning promotes vigorous, upright growth. Light pruning encourages branched, twiggy growth. Consider what you're trying to achieve before you cut.

When dead-heading summer-flowering Shrub roses, it's worth cutting back slightly further to keep the plants in shape; they will then need only a light prune in winter.

Rambler roses respond to more extensive summer pruning than other types of rose (*see* pages 60–3).

Autumn pruning

Rose pruning isn't essential in autumn, but it is desirable to give plants a tidy-up before winter. Remove damaged and diseased leaves and faded flowers, as for summer pruning, remembering not to dead-head roses that are going to produce hips.

Strong autumn winds can cause 'wind rock', which loosens the roses' roots in the soil and can damage plants. For this reason, if you're growing tall roses in exposed situations it's often recommended to cut back the shoots by one quarter to a third at this time. However, if the roses are well staked from the start, this isn't usually necessary.

Autumn is also a good time to tie in any long, unruly shoots of Climbing and Rambler roses (*see* page 61).

Quick-trim method

Recent trials have shown that the flowering performance of Shrub roses is just as good if you cut off the top of the bush using a hedge trimmer or pair of shears as if you prune in the traditional way, carefully removing individual stems. However, the problem with this approach is that you won't look at the plants closely and may not spot what needs to be done in terms of keeping the basic framework open and well spaced and removing dead and diseased wood as it develops. So it's better to do the job properly and methodically.

Pruning Shrub roses

Most Shrub roses have a bushy or arching habit and flower on the sideshoots produced near the ends of the main stems. If you hard prune them in the same way as Hybrid Tea and Floribunda roses, they'll produce upright, vigorous shoots that will be difficult to support, and may well produce flowers on shoots so tall that they're visible only from the first-floor bedroom windows. Also, these tall, vigorous shoots seem to be weaker in constitution and more susceptible to disease. What you want to create is a bushy shrub with plenty of side branches that will flower profusely at, or just below, eye and nose level. Prune in winter or early spring and dead-head the blooms after flowering.

Rugosa roses and some Species roses need little in the way of regular pruning. However, to avoid having a very upright plant with all the blooms and leaves on the top, they benefit from shaping to encourage a nice, rounded shrub form. To achieve this, cut some of the shoots on the outside of the shrub to one third lower than those in the middle.

Newly planted Shrub roses

Prune lightly, cutting back shoots by about one third, as for established roses (*see* above right). Many Shrub roses will flower for a number of years without any formal pruning.

Don't forget

Suckers are less common on Shrub roses than on Modern Bush roses, and they're also harder to identify. Take care when removing them, and if in doubt leave them until the rose is in leaf, when they will be easier to spot.

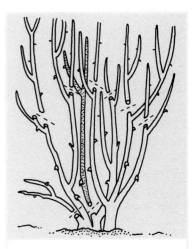

Prune Shrub roses in late winter or early spring, first removing dead, damaged, dying and diseased wood, then any suckers that are present. Cut back the remaining shoots by about one third to create an open, bushy shrub.

Established Shrub roses

When pruning mature Shrub roses, you'll probably need loppers or a pruning saw. Use loppers for stems up to about 2.5cm (1in) thick; for thicker branches, you may need to use a pruning saw (*see* page 57).

As with all pruning, start by removing any dead, dying, diseased and damaged wood. It pays to remove a few old, woody stems, cutting back to the base of the plant. This helps to space out the newer shoots and allows new growth to develop from the base of the plant. Next, carefully remove any suckers (*see* box, opposite).

Prune the remaining shoots by about one third. You're aiming for an open, bushy shrub with side branches on the main shoots. The finished height should be somewhere between knee and waist level in the case of shorter Shrub roses, such as 'Madame Knorr' and 'Jubilee Celebration', and between waist and chest height for taller-growing varieties, for example 'Maiden's Blush' and 'Penelope'.

Pruning Modern Bush roses

When pruning Modern Bush roses, the aim is to encourage an open, well-balanced, goblet-shaped plant that will allow good air circulation. This helps to avoid disease and damage caused by branches rubbing together. As many Modern Bush roses are less vigorous than Shrub roses, harder pruning is necessary to encourage vigorous growth and large, long-stemmed blooms.

Prune Modern Bush roses annually, in winter or early spring. Their small size makes them relatively easy to prune, and usually a pair of secateurs will be all that you

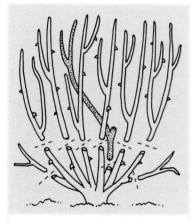

When pruning Modern Bush roses in late winter or early spring, as with Shrub roses remove dead, damaged, dying and diseased wood and suckers. Take out any branches that are crossing in the centre of the plant, then cut back by half to two thirds the stems you intend to keep.

Don't prune!

Some roses, such as the Rugosa roses, *Rosa moyesii* hybrids (above) and the Ramblers 'Rambling Rector' and 'Wedding Day', produce lovely red hips after the flowers have finished. Where this is the case, avoid pruning in summer or autumn after flowering, or you won't get any hips. Instead, prune in late winter, after the hips have finished.

need. Also, dead-head roses in summer (*see* pages 58–9). Patio roses need lighter pruning than Hybrid Teas or Floribundas. Follow the same procedure, but don't cut back as hard and leave more of the slender, twiggy growth intact.

Newly planted Modern Bush roses

If the roses are new, or planted within the last couple of years, cut the stems down to three or four buds above ground level, ideally making slanting cuts just above outward-facing buds to encourage an open centre.

Established Modern Bush roses

Cut out any dead, damaged, dying or diseased wood. Shrivelled, brown or broken shoots should be cut out completely, ideally to just above a bud or right to the base of the plant. Then remove any suckers (*see* page 58). Remove any branches that cross over and compete in the centre of

the plant and cut out weak and puny growth. Next, prune the main stems you're keeping. Cut back by half to two thirds of the original height of the plant, leaving it just below knee height, about 15–30cm (6–12in).

Pruning and training Climbing roses

Climbing roses are often tall forms of Hybrid tea, Floribunda and English roses. They're not climbers in the true sense of the word, as they can't support themselves, so you have to take control and train them. Training a rose horizontally means the roses produce a much better display, with flowers blooming along the entire length of the shoot rather than just on the end third (*see* pages 52 and 56). If you're training a Climbing rose up a vertical support, such as a pillar, make sure you tie in the stems in a spiral fashion (*see* page 54).

There are two main ways you can go wrong in the pruning of Climbing roses. If you cut back too hard at an early stage, they may never get going and decide to remain as unruly, sprawling shrubs rather than sending up strong, upright stems. Or you may be too cautious with mature plants. If you just snip and tidy you'll end up with woody, bare stems at the bottom and all the flowers and growth at the top. However, if you follow these instructions you can't go far wrong.

Don't forget

When you make a cut above a bud, remember that the bud will grow in the direction it is pointing in – this is useful when imagining how the plant will develop.

Newly planted Climbing roses

There's not usually any need for pruning in the first year after planting; just make sure you keep the shoots tied into the support. After the second summer, you should have some strong shoots that are long enough to bend over and tie in – horizontally along wires or spirally up a vertical support. Dead-head roses after flowering.

Don't forget

As part of the pruning process, clear up any leaf or stem debris from around the plants, and break up the surface of the soil with a hand fork or hoe. This helps to minimize disease by removing fungal spores and prepares the ground for fertilizer application.

In late winter or early spring, shorten the sideshoots of Climbing roses to two or three buds from the main stems to encourage the production of new flowering shoots.

HOW TO prune and train an established Climbing rose

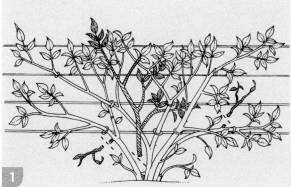

1

In autumn, prune out any old, unwanted wood before tying in the new season's stems. Start by removing any dead, damaged, dying or diseased branches, and thin out any congested growth or crossing stems from the centre of the plant. Removing the old, unproductive growth means that the rose can channel its energy into producing new, flowering shoots.

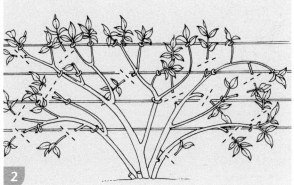

2

Train the new season's stems into the wire, bending the shoots a little to meet the wire. This horizontal training will encourage more flowers. In late winter or early spring, cut back these sideshoots again to two or three buds from the main stems, remove weak and spindly growth and tie in any more upright shoots that have developed.

How and when to prune roses

Roses are pruned in different ways according to their type, and the chart below gives advice for each individual group. In all cases, remove dead, damaged, diseased or dying wood, suckers (*see* page 58) and blind shoots (*see* page 75). In areas with mild winters, carry out main pruning tasks in late winter, but in colder areas leave it until early spring. Dead-head all roses after flowering, except those that have attractive hips, which you should leave until midwinter. Miniature roses need only a very light trim, or they disappear!

GROUP	SEASON	HOW TO MAINTAIN ESTABLISHED ROSES
Hybrid Teas, Floribundas	Late winter to early spring	Remove weak, spindly stems and any branches that cross over and compete in the centre of the plant. Cut back main stems to just below knee height, around 15–30cm (6–12in).
	Summer to autumn	Dead-head at the end of each flush of flowers; cut back long, straggly shoots.
Shrub roses (all)	Late winter to early spring	Cut back stems by about one third; remove some old, woody stems, cutting back to the base of the plant.
Summer-flowering varieties	Summer	Dead-head after plants have completely finished blooming.
Repeat-flowering varieties	Summer to autumn	Dead-head at the end of each flush of flowers and again when the final display is over.
Patio and Ground-cover roses	Late winter to early spring	Nip off any ends of stems that have died back over winter and take out any weak, broken or overcrowded stems.
	Summer to autumn	Dead-head at the end of each flush of flowers.
Climbing roses	Autumn	Cut back old, unwanted stems to 30cm (12in) above ground level; tie in the new season's stems, training them horizontally, and any unruly shoots to prevent wind rock.
	Late winter to early spring	Cut back sideshoots to two or three buds from the main stems; remove weak, spindly growth and tie in upright shoots that have developed.
	Summer	Dead-head after flowering, if blooms are accessible.
Rambler roses	Summer (except those with hips)	After flowering, cut back flowered shoots to where new shoots are appearing lower down the plant. New shoots arise from the base.
	Autumn	Tie in long, unruly shoots to prevent wind rock.
	Late winter to early spring	Thin out shoots as necessary. On mature plants, cut back some of the old, woody stems right to the base of the plant.

Established Climbing roses

In summer, unless the rose is a very tall, rampant variety, dead-head the roses as the flowers fade. In autumn, cut out unwanted shoots before tying in the new season's stems, then in late winter or early spring cut back the new shoots to two or three buds (*see* page 61). This process ensures that, over several years, the oldest, least productive growth is gradually replaced by younger, more vigorous stems.

Pruning and training Rambler roses

Rambler roses are natural climbers that are adapted to scaling trees, shrubs or other forms of support. They do not need pruning for vigour, but it's worth removing the old, woody stems to ensure the rose remains healthy and to keep it within bounds if possible. Those that have found their home scaling a tree or smothering a building simply cannot be pruned unless you take really drastic action (*see* opposite). Pruning Ramblers is best tackled twice during the year: once straight after flowering in late summer (except for those roses with hips), and again in winter.

Don't forget

Rambler roses 'fight back' while they're being pruned, so beware of their thorns and wear plenty of protective clothing. Regular tetanus injections are advisable to eliminate the risk of infection through cuts in the skin.

Newly planted Rambler roses

In the first year or two, Rambler roses need little pruning apart from removing any faded flowerheads and dead wood. Tie in the shoots as they develop to point them in the direction you want them to grow. When planting bare-root roses in winter, cut back any long stems to about 45cm (18in) above soil level immediately after planting.

Established Rambler roses

After a Rambler has bloomed you'll see vigorous new shoots emerging from lower in the plant, behind the flowering shoots. Where possible, cut out the shoots that have flowered back to where those new shoots are growing from. This will channel the energy into the new growth, which will develop and bloom the following year. Tie in these shoots loosely as they grow; they can be fragile, so take care. In winter or early spring, thin out shoots as necessary. Remove any shoots that have flowered, or cut back the sideshoots on young flowered shoots in the same way that you would treat a Climbing rose (*see* page 61).

On mature plants, it's worth cutting back some of the old woody stems right to the base of the plant to encourage new growth. You will need a pruning saw for this and a little brute strength.

Pruning neglected and rampant roses

A very overgrown rose, which has not been pruned for many years, may become a tangled mass of stems that grow weakly and produce

HOW TO renovate a rose in stages

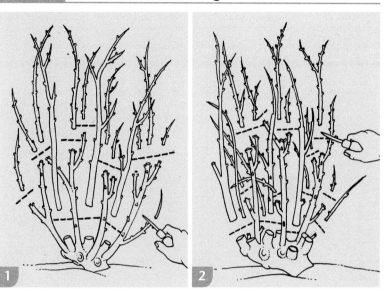

1 In autumn, ideally before leaf fall, cut out all dead, dying, diseased and damaged wood. In late winter, cut down to ground level half of the remaining stems (take away the oldest, thickest ones first). Shorten the rest by half and cut back the sideshoots to three or four buds. In summer, if large amounts of growth have been produced, thin out overcrowded shoots by removing every third one. Remove suckers by pulling them off at their point of origin (*see* box, page 58).

2 The following winter, remove all the old remaining stems that were not cut out last winter, as well as any diseased, damaged or unwanted shoots, to prevent overcrowding. Shorten the remaining shoots by half and cut back to three or four buds any sideshoots that formed on strong, vigorous stems produced during the growing season. In summer, again remove suckers, and cut back hard any blind shoots (*see* page 75) to stimulate lower buds into growth.

fewer, smaller flowers. It will also be more prone to pests and diseases because of the lack of air circulation around the plant. You may well be tempted to get rid of the rose and start again, but generally it's worth trying to renovate it. This means cutting it back hard to encourage new, vigorous shoots to grow.

Rampant Rambler roses can also be hard pruned. If they have grown up into large trees or shrubs and are inaccessible, it's impossible to prune them annually using conventional methods. While many can flower for

years without any attention, they may need to be dealt with at some point, for the sake of both the rose and the supporting tree or shrub. Every seven to ten years, in winter, you can cut them to within 50–75cm (20–30in) of ground level, and new shoots should replace those that have been removed.

Modern Bush and Shrub roses, Climbing roses and Rambler roses grown as Climbing roses, in a more controlled situation, are best renovated in stages, over a period of two years (*see* above).

A well-grown standard rose has an opulent charm: it can provide an impressive focal point in a garden, add a touch of formality to a bed or border, or make a dramatic subject for a large pot. A line of standard roses can be used to create an avenue effect along a path. The secret of successful standard roses is to choose good varieties that suit this type of training and grow them well.

A standard rose (here, the lovely repeat-flowering Shrub rose 'Ballerina') makes an attractive alternative to bay or other standard evergreens.

Standards are plants that are trained with a single, straight, branch-free stem or trunk and a rounded or weeping 'head' of branches. There are several different types and sizes of standard rose (see box, opposite).

A standard rose consists of two or three different roses that have been fused together to produce a bushy or trailing head on a long stem. The rootstock is usually one type of rose, the stem is another, which has been budded or grafted onto it (see box, page 68), and the head is the desired rose that has been budded, usually in three places around the top of the stem. Weeping standards are trained over an 'umbrella', or frame, on top of the support stake. The shoots are tied to this in winter and throughout the growing season to create a mushroom-like effect.

Planting a standard rose

Standard roses require sheltered sites and should be avoided in exposed gardens. Strong winds can break the branches away from the main stem and cause devastation when the plants are in full leaf and flower.

Plant as for other roses (see pages 48–50), but to protect the standard from wind it's vital to provide good support at the planting stage. The stake should be 2.5–5cm (1–2in) thick and placed on the side of the prevailing wind (although avoid planting a stake in front of the standard). Use strong tree ties to attach the stake to the stem. These must have spacers to keep the stem of the rose and the stake apart, otherwise the stem will rub against the stake and become damaged. Check these regularly – they should be tight but not restricting the flow of sap.

If growing standard roses in pots, choose large containers filled with loam-based potting compost.

Aftercare

Standard roses need regular attention during the growing season to keep them looking good. They require watering and feeding, just as other roses do (see page 51). Regular dead-heading helps to promote flower bud production, and remember that faded flowers are all the more visible on a standard. Any suckers that appear from the ground or on the stem must always be removed (see box, page 58).

Once established, bush standards usually need only a light pruning in winter to promote well-branched growth and lots of flowers. The pruning method will be the same as for those plants budded or grafted at

Don't forget

Always buy and plant the best-quality standard you can find. Look for a straight, strong, undamaged stem and a good number of shoots of similar vigour that will produce a balanced head with plenty of sideshoots and therefore masses of flowers.

ground level, so the 'head' on a Floribunda rose grown as a standard will be pruned in the same way as a Floribunda growing down at soil level. However, if during formation the head seems like it is becoming lopsided, you may need to hard prune the stems on the weak side to promote more vigorous growth.

Weeping standards need regular attention during the growing season. Cut out stems as the flowers fade and shorten any long shoots to keep them in bounds. In winter, thin remaining shoots and tie them into the framework, preserving healthy sideshoots and shortening these to within 30cm (12in) of the main stems.

Staking standard roses

When planting a standard, drive a stout hardwood or pressure-treated softwood stake into the ground to a depth of 50–60cm (20–24in). The support should reach the point where the head joins the stem. Use two small but strong tree ties, one halfway up the stem and one just below the head.

Don't forget

The secret of success when growing a standard rose is to provide adequate support. Remember that roses do not grow naturally like this. The gardener is balancing a heavy bush on a single stem that was never intended to support so many leaves and flowers.

The English rose 'Graham Thomas' makes a striking focal point grown as a standard.

How and where to use standard roses

There are several types of standard rose, which vary in height, vigour and shape. All are useful as specimen plants, but their size will determine where they will look best, in the garden or in a pot.

Miniature standards are also available, with an overall height of 60cm (2ft), but they're less common than patio standards and are very delicate creatures.

TYPE OF STANDARD	SIZE OF STANDARD	TYPE OF ROSE USED FOR THE 'HEAD'	WHERE TO PLANT	GOOD VARIETIES	NOTES
Patio standard (half-standard)	Stem 80cm (32in) Overall height 1–2m (3–4ft)	Patio roses, compact Floribundas, Ground-cover roses	Small bed or in a container	'Flower Carpet Pink' 'Flower Carpet White' 'Greenall's Glory' 'Queen Mother' 'Sweet Dream'	Flowers freely and repeat flowers well. Underplant with low-growing perennials, lavenders, herbs and silver foliage shrubs (see page 34)
Classic standard (full standard)	Stem 1–1.2m (3–4ft) Overall height 1.5m (5ft)	Modern Bush and Shrub roses	Medium-sized border or in a container beside the front door	'Ballerina' 'Brave Heart' 'Darcey Bussell' 'Golden Celebration' 'Graham Thomas' 'Iceberg' 'Margaret Merril'	Floribundas and English roses produce particularly full heads with plenty of flowers. Grow with other Modern Bush roses or lower-growing shrubs and perennials
Weeping standard	Stem 1.2–1.5m (4–5ft) Overall height 1.5–1.8m (5–6ft), with stems trailing to 60cm (2ft) above ground level	Climbing, Rambler and Ground-cover roses	Large border, alongside a path or as a specimen in a lawn	'Albéric Barbier' 'Félicité Perpétué' 'Flower Carpet Pink' 'Flower Carpet White'	Requires regular input from the gardener and does take up a lot of ground space; allow a circle of 2m (6ft) in diameter that can be planted with low-growing ground-cover plants

Propagating roses

The commercial budding of roses has led many gardeners to believe that roses can't grow on their own roots. In fact, most will and they're relatively easy to propagate, although you'll see more of the rose's individual peculiarities in terms of shapes, sizes and growth habits. Taking cuttings is an excellent way to make more of your favourite varieties or acquire desirable specimens from fellow gardeners, and it's very satisfying too. You can also propagate some roses by layering or by seed, although these methods aren't suitable for all roses.

Taking cuttings

It's possible to propagate all types of rose in this way, although be aware that there are restrictions (*see* box, page 68). Ideally, take rose cuttings any time from late spring to late summer, when the wood is semi-ripe, which means the shoots are green and fairly stiff but still flexible. Use a sharp garden knife or secateurs. It's important to remove the growing-tip, because this is soft and can be prone to wilting and disease, and if flower buds are present they may detract from root formation. Trimming the foliage helps to reduce water loss and keep the cutting alive. You can dip the ends of the shoot in water and then into a hormone rooting powder if you wish. This can help root formation but isn't essential.

Once the cuttings have rooted, those started between late spring and midsummer can be knocked out of the first container and separated and potted up individually. Those started in late summer are best left until the following spring. Grow them on in the pots outside or in a cold frame and plant them out the following season.

You can often root pieces of stem of cut roses on the windowsill in pots in the same way. Sometimes roses that you buy as cut flowers come with sideshoots that make ideal cutting material.

Propagating by layering

Roses with lax, spreading branches, such as Ramblers, Ground-cover roses and some types of Shrub rose, can be propagated by layering. This

HOW TO take rose cuttings

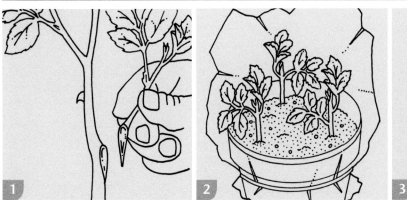

1 Take a cutting about 15–20cm (6–8in) long from the parent plant. You can take these with a heel (where a sideshoot meets the main stem), or from the end of a shoot. In the latter case, make a straight, clean cut just below a node. Remove the growing-tip and all the lower leaves. Leave two or three leaves at the top of the stem, shortening them to between two and four leaflets.

2 Root the cuttings in the open ground, in a shady, sheltered corner, or in a cold frame. Alternatively, push cuttings around the edge of a pot filled with multipurpose compost with some added sand or grit. Bury the lower third of the cutting in the compost and firm gently in place. Water the pot well and place it in a polythene bag with a few air holes. Remove the bag after about three weeks.

3 Place the pot in a sheltered corner of the garden or in a cold frame and keep it out of direct sunlight. Once the cuttings have rooted, in about two months' time, pot them up separately. Don't be tempted to plant the rooted cuttings straight out into the garden beds, as they won't be tough enough to survive. Grow them on in pots until they are approximately the same size as you'd buy them in the shops.

is an extremely simple way to propagate one or two plants from an established garden specimen. Roses that are suitable for layering include 'Albéric Barbier', 'Albertine', 'François Juranville', 'William Lobb' and 'Complicata'.

Growing roses from seed

Raising roses from seed isn't difficult, but it's not suitable for hybrid roses, as they won't come true from seed. However, Species roses will produce offspring that are the same as the parent, and it's a good way to raise Rugosa roses and Species roses grown for their hips. Miniature roses are often grown from seed, from

The very vigorous, single, pink rose 'Complicata', with its arching shoots and greyish-green leaves, can be propagated by layering.

HOW TO propagate roses by layering

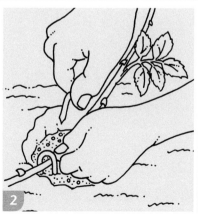
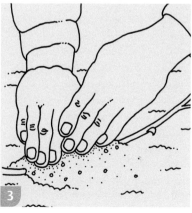

Choose a flexible shoot that will bend down to the ground. About 30–40cm (12–16in) or so from the end of the shoot, remove the leaves and cut 5cm (2in) of bark from the underside, using a sharp knife, to a depth of only 1–2mm (^{1}/16in). Take care not to sever the shoot.

Bend the shoot onto the ground. Where the wounded part touches the soil, break up the ground beneath with a trowel or hand fork and make a shallow depression. Anchor the shoot into the depression by pegging it down using a looped piece of stout, galvanized wire.

Cover the layered stem with soil, then water it thoroughly and leave it to root. This will usually take about three months. Detach the new shoot from the parent plant, cutting just before the layer. Pot up the new plant or transplant it directly to its new location.

To encourage seeds to germinate, place them in a warm spot and cover the pot with a plastic bag to create a humid environment.

Budding or grafting

When you buy a rose from a garden centre or nursery it will have been propagated by budding or grafting, which means the bud or stem of one rose will have been joined onto the roots of another. The advantage of propagating roses in this way is that the nurseryman can make a lot of plants from one individual over a few seasons.

All the roses produced in this way will be uniform in habit, of equal size and ready to sell at the same time. This method is more for the grower's than the gardener's convenience, but it is also true that the rootstock can add desirable characteristics to the finished rose: it may restrict the size of very vigorous varieties or provide strength to weak growers, and in some cases the rootstock helps with disease-resistance.

However, there is a downside for the gardener. Rootstocks are liable to produce their own growth shoots, known as suckers, which compete with the desired rose if they aren't removed (*see* box, page 58). You could also argue that the rootstock imposes its own qualities and you can't tell what the rose would be like if left to grow naturally.

garden mixtures rather than individual, named varieties. These seeds can be bought in packets like any other flower seed.

How to propagate roses from seed

If you want to try to propagate roses from seed, wait for the hips to ripen fully. At this stage, they will have turned from green to orange or red and they will appear slightly soft to the touch. Split them open with a sharp knife, taking care not to damage the seeds inside. Scrape them out carefully onto a piece of damp kitchen paper, fold this up and place it in a plastic bag. Put the bag containing the seeds into the bottom of the fridge.

After two months, take out the bag and sow the seeds in a pot containing seed compost, covering the seeds to a depth of about 6mm (¼in) with vermiculite or more

Some roses with hips, such as *Rosa rugosa*, will come true from seed, producing offspring that resemble the parent.

Don't forget

Bottom heat will help seeds to germinate more quickly, so use a heated propagator if you have one. Alternatively, cover the pots with a sheet of glass, clear acrylic or a plastic bag and put them on a sunny windowsill.

compost. Keep them warm and moist to encourage germination.

As soon as the seeds have germinated, move them to a cool, light position. Prick them out into individual 10–12cm (4–5in) pots of multipurpose compost. They will usually grow up and produce flowers in approximately six to eight weeks. At this stage, you can see what you have got, and decide what is worth keeping and what you should dispose of.

Understanding rose breeding

Roses grown in the wild, known as species roses, usually have a simple beauty, designed to attract pollinating insects so the flowers can go on to reproduce. Sometimes the offspring display different qualities, such as larger or more colourful flowers with more petals and a stronger fragrance. Over the years, many of these attractive variants have been introduced into our gardens and, in the quest to further improve upon nature, plant breeders have cross-pollinated numerous cultivars to produce a huge range of garden hybrids. Today, fuelled by demand from gardeners, ever-increasing numbers of roses are bred for their ornamental qualities, greater disease-resistance and easy-to-manage habit.

The award-winning English rose 'Gertrude Jekyll' has been bred for its large, rosette-shaped blooms and reliability.

Rose breeding is a slow process – it can take 10 years from pollination to a rose variety becoming available to buy at a nursery or garden centre. Only a handful of rose seedlings out of hundreds of thousands from a year's sowings make it to the marketplace. It involves several stages, requiring a lot of input on the part of the breeder.

Pollination
When the bloom of a parent plant is approaching its peak, the petals are removed, along with any stamens (the male part of the flower), leaving the stigma (the female part) exposed. This is the seed parent flower. The stamens from the other parent are then removed and pollen is transferred to the stigma of the seed parent. The flowerhead is covered with a bag.

Sowing the seed
Inside the bag the seedhead develops and ripens. When the seed is ripe, the hip is split open, the seeds are removed and are sown in a greenhouse. The seeds germinate and grow and each seedling produces a single bloom in

about six to eight weeks. The breeder selects those that show promise in terms of colour, shape and fragrance.

Producing the crop
A bud or stem (known as budwood) is taken from the selected seedlings and budded onto rootstocks in the field (*see* box, opposite). Each seedling will yield about three plants. If these still show promise in the field, a trial batch of nine or ten plants will be

grown; these will be carefully monitored for performance, stability and weather- and disease-resistance. After five or six years, once the breeder is quite certain that the variety will be a winner, increasing numbers will be budded each year until a realistic number of plants have been produced to launch the new rose on the market.

Many roses, including Hybrid Teas and Floribundas, are bred purely for cutting. Most are happy outdoors but some prefer the protection of a greenhouse.

Rose problems and remedies

Roses are renowned for being prone to disease and attack by pests. It can be very disheartening, when you've looked forward to beautiful flowers all winter, to go out into the garden and discover greenfly have smothered and disfigured the buds and foliage before you've had time to enjoy them. Prevention is always more effective than cure, so keep plants healthy and if problems do occur deal with them straight away.

Preventing rose problems

If you grow healthy roses, and look after your plants well, you're going a long way towards preventing problems from happening in the first place. Here are a few good practices that will help.

■ Grow disease-resistant varieties. Progress has been made in recent years in developing more disease-resistant roses. If you have roses that frequently struggle, always get disease and never please, maybe it's time to dig them up, dispose of them and buy some new ones.

■ Avoid planting a rose where another has been removed in the past few years, as this can cause rose replant sickness (*see* page 74).

■ Growing roses in combination with various other plants rather than in a dedicated rose bed will help protect them from devastation by one particular pest or disease.

■ It's vital to establish a natural, healthy ecosystem, so encourage beneficial insects to your garden (*see* box, opposite).

■ Keep a watchful eye and pick off diseased leaves as soon as they show signs of infection. This is the time to spray if you're going to, rather than waiting until the disease has spread all over the plant.

■ Practise good hygiene around the plants. Clean up any fallen leaves,

petals and pruning debris during summer and especially in winter. This is where fungal spores hide and wait to recolonize your roses.

■ Feed your roses regularly in spring and again in summer to promote healthy foliage and vigorous growth. Roses that are struggling in poor soil are more susceptible to disease.

■ Water your roses in dry weather and mulch in winter or spring with organic matter to help conserve moisture in the soil. Roses that are dry at the roots are more susceptible to attack by mildew.

■ Prune carefully in winter to develop plants with an open branch structure that will allow good air circulation through the foliage (*see* pages 57–63). This helps to move any fungal spores on, rather than allowing them to settle and colonize.

Identifying the cause

Even the most diligent gardeners experience problems with their roses. The first step to dealing with a problem is to identify the cause. All too often, out of desperation, a gardener will reach for a rose spray and find that it makes no difference whatsoever, as the problem has been incorrectly identified and the wrong treatment has been applied to the rose. To diagnose a problem and decide on the appropriate

Biological control

A biological control is when you add a natural predator to control a pest. The predator is normally added in the larval stage, and when released it feeds on the pest. This method of pest control works really well in an enclosed environment, such as a greenhouse, but is less useful in the open garden. However, if you garden organically and avoid chemicals you can introduce the larvae of ladybirds (above) and lacewings to boost the population of these beneficial insects.

course of action, you first need to determine whether the problem is the result of a pest, a disease or a physiological disorder.

Pests (*see* pages 72–3) These are insects or other animals that cause damage to a plant. They can harm or destroy any part of a plant or even the whole plant by feeding in various ways, or by causing abnormal growths known as galls. Some pests damage plants by spreading viral or fungal diseases (*see* below). Where possible, a barrier should be created to prevent the pest from getting to the plant; alternatively, you can sometimes remove them by hand; as a last resort, roses can be treated with a pesticide, ideally an organic type (*see* opposite).

Diseases (*see* pages 74–5) Plant diseases are caused by other organisms, such as fungi, bacteria and viruses. In most cases, diseases are fungal; bacterial diseases are relatively rare. Diseases can cause considerable damage, usually to the flowers and foliage, and the growth or health of the plant is invariably affected. Ideally, diseases will be avoided by cultural techniques that help prevent the disease from developing on the plant in the first place. However, if it's too late they can be treated with a fungicide.

Disorders (*see* page 75) can be caused by lack of a nutrient or nutrients in the soil, by poor cultivation methods and unsuitable atmospheric conditions. They can cause discoloration of the foliage, stem wilt, and disfigurement of the flowers, and unless correctly diagnosed and treated can reduce vigour, sometimes killing the plant. Deficiencies are often confused with diseases, but they can usually be treated by correct feeding, watering and mulching with organic matter.

Beating the bugs

Even the most well-cared-for roses can become a martyr to insect pests. In many cases, you can remove them without resorting to sprays. Larger creatures, such as caterpillars, can be removed by hand. In the case of smaller insects, such as aphids or froghoppers, you can use a high-pressure jet of water from a hose to dislodge them from roses.

As a last resort you may want to use an insecticide. Try to avoid using chemical sprays whenever possible, as they can be damaging to the environment and may eradicate beneficial insects. The development of resistance in some insects also means that chemical controls are not always as effective as you think. There are now many organic treatments available, based on natural ingredients, as well as biological controls for many pests (*see* box, opposite).

If using a pesticide, ensure that the product you choose will do the job required. Indiscriminate use of any pesticide – organic or non-organic – is inadvisable because it will affect harmless and beneficial insects as well as the bad guys. Understand what you're using, and use it very carefully, following the instructions to the letter.

There are several types of pesticides, which all work in different ways:

Contact insecticides These can be organic or chemical and work only when they touch the insect, so you must spray very carefully.

Systemic insecticides These are chemical, and are absorbed into the plant and remain in the sap stream for a few weeks. These are effective at controlling sap-sucking insects. You don't necessarily have to get the pesticide on the insect – it can come into contact with it when it feeds.

Combined products In recent years, the trend has been to use combined insecticide and fungicide sprays, often with a foliar feed for good measure. These are convenient, but you may be using a chemical when you don't need one. If you have mildew and no aphids, why put on an insecticide when all you need is a fungicide?

Rose pests

Ants

On dry, well-drained soils, ants often make their nest by tunnelling along the roots of a rose bush, which can cause poor growth and performance because of disruption to the roots. Ants 'farm' aphids for their honeydew, so where you see ants you may also discover aphids.

Prevention and control Keep the soil damp so the ants go elsewhere. They also dislike the smell of mint, so planting it around the roses can help to deter them.

Aphids

Often referred to as greenfly, aphids are sap-sucking insects that distort and damage young rose shoots and flower buds, particularly in early summer. They also excrete sticky honeydew, which encourages black sooty mould.

Prevention and control Tackle aphids as soon as they appear, before populations build up. Spray with a sharp jet of water to dislodge the pests or rub off aphids with your fingers for small infestations. If necessary, spray with an organic pesticide based on plant extracts, such as pyrethrum, soft or insecticidal soap or plant oils. As a very last resort use a chemical-based spray. Encourage beneficial insects, such as ladybirds and lacewings, to the garden as they feed on aphids.

Caterpillars

Several types of caterpillar attack roses, causing irregular-shaped holes in the leaves. If the leaves are rolled and webbed as well, the damage will be due to the tortrix moth caterpillar.

Prevention and control Caterpillars are not a big problem on roses. If damage is slight and only a few caterpillars are involved, simply pick off the culprits. For greater infestations, you could use pyrethrum spray.

Chafer grubs and beetles

Adult chafer beetles cause irregular damage to rose foliage in early summer. The large, creamy-white grubs live below the ground and feed on the roots, which will weaken the plant and can eventually kill it.

Prevention and control Usually a problem on light, sandy soils, both chafer grubs and beetles are difficult to control. A soil drench with a suitable biological control may be partially successful. As a last resort, a systemic insecticide helps to control the beetles.

Froghoppers

These yellow-green insects produce clusters of white, foamy bubbles (known as 'cuckoo spit') on the green shoots, often just below the buds and flowers in late spring and early summer. The leaves may wilt – a sign of stress – but normally the effect is unsightly rather than damaging.

Prevention and control Usually a strong jet of water will dislodge the froghoppers and foam, or wipe them off by hand.

Leaf-cutter bees

Leaf-cutter bees are harmless industrious insects that make round, regularly shaped holes around the edge of leaves and use the leaf discs to line their tunnels. In severe cases, they can remove most of the leaf-blades, leaving only the midribs. You may find these bees in the space between bricks, in a gap under a window ledge or in a flowerpot.

Prevention and control No control is necessary. The rose will soon produce new foliage.

Leaf-rolling sawfly

This pest specifically attacks roses. If you see rose leaflets rolled tightly and hanging down, unroll them and you will find the pale green grub of the rose leaf-rolling sawfly growing inside. The leaves may shrivel and dry out.

Prevention and control Cut off the affected leaves and dispose of them or squeeze the rolled leaves to squash the larvae. Keep the soil under plants well weeded in winter to expose the overwintering larvae to predators.

Red spider mite
Usually associated with plants grown under glass, red spider mite can be a problem outside in hot, dry weather. It is most common on roses growing against sunny, south-facing walls. Leaves look pale and discoloured or slightly bronze and lack lustre. In severe attacks, fine webbing is visible around the leaf-stalks.
Prevention and control Spraying regularly with water, particularly the undersides of leaves, helps to maintain humidity and reduce the spread of the pest. Spray with plant oils or fatty acids as soon as the trouble is spotted. As a last resort use an insecticide that specifies that it controls red spider mite.

Rose galls
There are several different types of gall, which appear as irregular lumps on leaves, stems and roots. They are usually caused by small, burrowing insect pests, which inhabit these strange growths. Robin's pincushion (shown right) is a mossy, red or green growth that sometimes appears on rose leaves, particularly on species roses. Like most galls, these are harmless, but they may be considered unsightly. The only ones to worry about are crown galls, which can appear on the roots. These are brown, corky and can affect the growth of the plant.
Prevention and control The only method of control for crown galls is to cut out the infected plant parts.

Rose leafhopper
Small, yellow insects feed on leaf sap and cause mottling in patches on the surface of the leaves. Close inspection may reveal the skins they have shed on the underside of the foliage. The leaves become pale and the rose may appear to lack vigour.
Prevention and control Pick off the larvae. Spray with an organic treatment such as pyrethrum, fatty acids or plant oils in early or mid-spring, before infestations take off. As a last resort, spray upper and lower leaf surfaces with insecticide.

Rose scale
Rose scale is usually grey and mealy and forms patches of small, mound-like structures on old stems. It is unsightly and weakens growth. Scale is difficult to control because the insects that cause it are protected under their hard outer casings.

Prevention and control Cut out infected stems or wipe off the scale using kitchen roll soaked in soft soap or diluted washing-up liquid. As a last resort, drench with an insecticide spray that specifies control of scale.

Rose slugworm
This feeds by scraping off the outer tissues of leaves, leaving a 'skeleton' behind that soon dries off and turns brown. It is not common and rarely does extreme damage; normally only a few leaves are affected.
Prevention and control Examine the foliage carefully and pick off the greenish grubs if possible. If necessary, spray with a pyrethum-based insecticide. As a last resort, spray upper and lower sides of the leaves with an insecticide.

Thrips
Commonly known as thunder flies, thrips are tiny, winged insects that feed by burrowing into developing leaves and buds, which become mottled and distorted. The edges of petals can also become blackened, particularly on thin-petalled roses. Thrips cause most damage from early summer to early autumn.
Prevention and control Keep plants well watered and spray with organic pesticide, such as pyrethrum, if necessary to control numbers.

Rose diseases

Black spot

This is one of the most widespread and serious problems of roses. Fuzzy-edged, black spots, often edged with yellow, appear on the foliage from early summer onwards. These spread rapidly and cause leaves to yellow and fall. The condition is often worse in damp weather and is at its worst in midsummer. Some roses are more susceptible than others, so choose resistant types whenever possible.

Prevention and control Pick off any diseased leaves as soon as they appear and dispose of them along with any fallen leaves. Black spot is thought to be made worse by potash deficiency, so feed with a high-potash fertilizer. Mulch to stop spores splashing up from the ground. If black spot is a recurring problem, as a last resort you could spray with a fungicide at the first signs of disease and continue to spray regularly during the season.

Rose canker

This is a fungal infection that causes brown patches low down on the stems. These patches can spread and kill the infected stems.

Prevention and control Cut out infected stems and dispose of them. This may mean cutting back to soil level. Stems can be made more susceptible to canker through damage, so take care when cultivating around the plants.

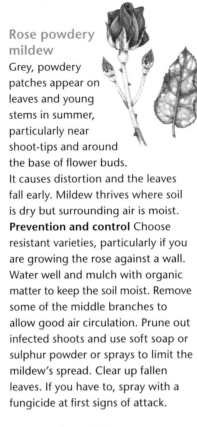

Rose powdery mildew

Grey, powdery patches appear on leaves and young stems in summer, particularly near shoot-tips and around the base of flower buds. It causes distortion and the leaves fall early. Mildew thrives where soil is dry but surrounding air is moist.

Prevention and control Choose resistant varieties, particularly if you are growing the rose against a wall. Water well and mulch with organic matter to keep the soil moist. Remove some of the middle branches to allow good air circulation. Prune out infected shoots and use soft soap or sulphur powder or sprays to limit the mildew's spread. Clear up fallen leaves. If you have to, spray with a fungicide at first signs of attack.

Rose replant sickness

A newly planted rose struggles to establish and fails to grow; this may be because a rose was grown in this situation previously. The cause is thought to be eelworms transmitting viruses, but it may also be fungal infections. (*See also* box, page 50.)

Prevention and control Ideally, avoid planting a rose where another has been removed in the past few years. If this is not possible, remove the existing soil, taking away an area at least 45cm (18in) square and deep, and and replace it with new. When planting, add mycorrhizal fungal granules and nitrogen-based fertilizer to the base of the planting hole and feed new roses regularly.

Rose rust

This fungal disease usually appears from midsummer onwards and can be very severe. It produces clusters of orange spores on the leaf undersides and yellow-orange spots on the upper surfaces; the leaves fall early and vigour is reduced. The stems may be infected with crusty scabs that cause cracking in the bark, which allow in secondary infections. A severe attack can cause dieback of the stems.

Prevention and control Prune out early signs of rust. Mulch and remove fallen leaves to prevent reinfection. Spores may overwinter on supports, so consider changing these. As a last resort, spray upper and lower surfaces with a fungicide recommended for rust. Keep up spraying until late summer.

Rose viruses

Rose viruses can cause yellow veining of the leaves or a pattern of light and dark areas. Plants may be stunted or distorted.

Prevention and control Viruses are spread by sap-sucking insects, mainly aphids, which is one major reason to control these pests (*see* page 72). Once a rose is infected there is nothing you can do; live with it or remove it. Inadvertent weedkiller damage can produce similar effects (*see* box, below right).

Rose disorders

Blind shoots

These are shoots that produce leaves that are often smaller than normal, and end in what appears to be the remains of a bud but one that does not develop and bloom. Some varieties seem to be particularly susceptible, especially if the rose is growing weakly. Blind shoots are also more common on roses growing in shade.

Prevention and control The best treatment is to feed the rose and cut back the shoot by half to two thirds above a healthy leaf. This will stimulate growth of a new shoot, which should flower normally.

Bud balling

Flower buds develop normally, but the flowers fail to open. The petals appear stuck together and often turn brown at the edges. Usually only a few buds are affected and plants remain healthy otherwise. Roses with many thin petals are especially susceptible to bud balling.

Prevention and control Balling occurs when warm, wet weather is followed by sunshine, so prevention is difficult. When watering roses, avoid doing so in the evenings and take care to direct the water at the roots, not over the plant. Remove affected buds to prevent dieback.

Proliferation

Leaves and buds grow through the middle of an existing flower, and a new flower may form above the first, causing deformity. The older, summer-flowering Shrub roses are particularly prone to this. It can be made worse by cool weather and temperature variations.

Prevention and control There is nothing you can do about it. Cut out affected flowers if they offend you.

Other disorders

Some problems are caused by poor management or nutrient deficiencies, and occasionally these are mistaken for a disease. It's important you recognize these symptoms so you treat them correctly – there's no point in treating plants with fungicide if all they need is to be fed and watered.

■ Nutrient deficiencies cause discoloration of rose foliage. This may manifest itself as reddish-brown or purple spotting, brown edges to the leaves or yellowing between the veins, according to the nutrient that is deficient. However, the identification of the missing nutrient is largely irrelevant as the simple solution is always the same. Apply a balanced rose fertilizer and water thoroughly (*see* page 51).

■ Purple spotting is often confused with black spot (*see* opposite), but the spots are small and irregular, and don't result in yellowing and leaf drop. It is caused by lack of nutrients and poor growing conditions, so feed, water and mulch regularly (*see* pages 46 and 51).

■ Weedkiller damage caused by spray drift, vapourized herbicide on warm air or contaminated stable manure can cause twisting of the leaf-stalks and narrow, distorted leaves. This is often mistaken for viral infection (*see* opposite). However, if the damage is from herbicide, the rose will recover and grow normally in a few weeks.

10 tips for safe spraying

If you have to use a spray, whether organic or inorganic, make sure you use it carefully to reduce damage to the environment, plants, people and animals. Always take the following precautions:

1 Choose the most appropriate product; make sure it is the right one for the job.

2 Always apply the spray at the dilution rate and frequency suggested by the manufacturer. Never mix chemicals.

3 Spray early in the morning or late in the evening. Few bees and other beneficial insects are around at this time, so you run less risk of harming them. Also, as it's cooler then, pesticide will stay on the foliage rather than evaporate.

4 Choose a still day and use a medium-droplet spray rather than a fine one; this is less likely to drift if there is air movement.

5 Moisten the upper and lower surfaces of the leaf thoroughly; ideally, the nozzle should be around 15–20cm (6–8in) away from the foliage as you spray.

6 Avoid spraying the inside of open flowers, as this can cause harm to beneficial insects.

7 Mix up the exact volume of spray that you need, and use it as soon as possible after spraying. Don't store solution.

8 Never use old or out-of-date chemicals or those that have been withdrawn.

9 Do not inhale sprays, avoid contact with skin and eyes, and keep children and pets away when applying.

10 Never tip unwanted chemicals down the drain. Even if there's only a small amount, dilute it and water it thinly over gravel or vacant ground. For larger quantities, consult your local authority for advice.

Rose care calendar

During the course of the year your roses need your input. When in full growth and flower in midsummer, they demand plenty of attention if you're to keep them in tip-top condition. Once you've put them to bed for the winter, there is less to do until you prune them. This calendar, or checklist, will help to remind you what you should be doing and when, but remember that timings vary according to the weather and from one part of the country to another.

Dead-head roses often during the growing season. Removing the spent blooms will encourage more flowers.

Early to mid-spring

■ Check roses that were planted in autumn to make sure that they're still firm in the ground. Firm them in with your heel if frost or wind has loosened them over the winter.

■ This is your last chance to plant new, bare-root roses.

■ Prune any Modern Bush roses that have not already been attended to.

■ Feed all roses with a granular rose fertilizer, sprinkling it over the soil around the plants and gently mixing it into the soil surface.

■ Mulch roses with manure or garden compost. This is also the time to mulch with chipped bark if you're using it as a weed suppressant and to conserve moisture.

In summer, keep an eye out for black spot, one of the most frequently occurring fungal diseases of roses.

■ Put supports for tall Shrub roses in place and check supports for Climbing roses to ensure they're able to cope with the weight of growth as the season progresses.

Late spring

■ Look out for early signs of insect pests and diseases. Pick off any affected leaves at the first signs of attack and spray with a suitable pesticide if necessary.

■ Weed around the roses, ensuring there is no competition from other, unwanted plants.

■ Ensure that surrounding shrubs and perennials do not swamp roses as they grow, cutting or tying back conflicting shoots and branches.

■ Roses growing in pots will now need regular watering until late autumn. This should be daily during hot weather.

Early summer

■ If the weather is dry, water roses to help support expanding foliage and flowers.

■ Tie up Shrub, Climbing and Rambler roses as necessary as the weight of flowers increases.

■ Dead-head roses as the blooms fade to encourage new flowers.

■ Look out for signs of fungal disease – particularly black spot and mildew. You may need to spray regularly with a fungicide.

■ This is a good time to buy and plant containerized roses to fill gaps in the garden. The plants are in bud or flower so are easy to place in the right colour combinations in the border.

Midsummer

■ Dead-head roses. Usually the first flush of roses is coming to an end, so it's the time to tidy up Shrub and Modern Bush roses by removing faded flower clusters.

■ Feed roses with another application of granular fertilizer.

■ Water roses thoroughly if the ground is dry.

■ Continue to spray regularly against fungal diseases. Look out for signs of rust (*see* page 74) and pick off any infected leaves.

Late summer

■ Keep dead-heading roses. Repeat-flowering rose varieties bloom well at this time if you fed them earlier in the season.

■ Prune Rambler roses now. Look for where new shoots are emerging lower on the stems and cut back the stems that have flowered to this point.

■ Remove any annual weeds before they set seed, otherwise they will colonize the ground around the roses next spring.

Early autumn

■ Enjoy late blooms and dead-head spent flowers regularly to keep roses looking good.

■ Spray with a fungicide against late rust attacks if necessary; if left untreated, rust can cause dieback of the stems.

■ Clean up any leaf debris around the plants – this can harbour fungal spores over winter.

Mid- to late autumn

■ This is the ideal time to plant new roses, whether they're bare-root or containerized plants. The soil is

Autumn is the perfect time to plant roses. Prepare the ground thoroughly before planting, adding plenty of organic matter to improve the soil texture.

Whatever time of year you need to prune, dead-head or shorten a stem, always cut just above a bud.

warm and moist, and they have all winter to get established. Prepare the ground thoroughly before you plant, forking in organic matter.

■ Shorten back the growth of tall varieties in exposed situations to prevent damage by wind.

■ Tie in any stray stems on Climbing and Rambler roses.

Winter

■ You can continue to plant new roses throughout the winter, providing that the ground is not frozen. If bare-root roses arrive and the ground is not suitable for planting, heel them in and postpone planting until the weather improves.

■ Prune Shrub and English roses in late winter or early spring. Climbing

and Modern Bush roses can be pruned at the same time in all but the coldest areas.

■ Sort out, train and tie in new stems of Climbing roses.

Tie in the long shoots of Climbing and Rambler roses if necessary to protect them from wind damage.

Recommended roses

The popularity of roses all over the world has inspired rose breeders to produce thousands of varieties for you to choose from – and that list gets longer every year! Choosing a rose for your garden can be a difficult task; after all, it's not just a matter of selecting the colour you want. You will also want to consider growth habit, flower shape, fragrance and disease-resistance, at the very least. This directory should help you; it contains some of the most reliable varieties that are available from rose nurseries, garden centres and via mail order.

A–Z directory

This directory is organized by rose type, and the varieties in each section are listed alphabetically. The selection is made on the basis of reliability, good health and all-round garden performance, as well as aesthetic quality. Some widely grown, popular varieties have been omitted because they fall short in disease-resistance and tolerance of various growing conditions.

Choosing roses

There is always something that first attracts us to a plant, and this is certainly true of a rose. It might be the flower's colour and shape, or its rich fragrance. However, an even more important consideration is where you will use the plant. How big does it get? Will it thrive in a slightly shady site? Will it suit the style of your garden? For example, some roses are free spirits that are at home in naturalistic gardens, while a well-tempered Hybrid Tea rose or a compact English rose would be far more appropriate in a neat, formal garden. Maybe you want roses for cutting for the house, or to plant as a hedge? There is a rose for every garden, and every gardener.

KEY to symbols

In this chapter the following symbols are used to indicate qualities that a rose is particularly noted for. A rough idea is also given as to the plant's height (H) and spread (S) under good growing conditions and a regime of pruning that is in line with that recommended in this book.

- ◖ Tolerates some shade
- ◌ Tolerates poor, dry soil
- ◯ Reliably disease-resistant
- ✳ Strongly or deliciously fragrant
- ❖ Flowering season (hips when relevant)

Growing conditions

Gardeners with less than ideal soil conditions can usually improve matters with good cultivation, but some poor soils are hard to improve and then it's best to choose one of the more tolerant varieties. Most Gallica, Alba and Rugosa roses are tough and tolerant of poor, dry soils. Roses like sun, but a variety noted here as shade-tolerant, often a Rugosa, a Hybrid Musk or an English rose, should succeed in less than the four hours' direct sun that is the ideal for most roses. (*See* pages 120–1.)

Disease-resistance

Few roses are completely free from disease throughout their lives. Even the healthiest can suffer from a little black spot or mildew in a poor growing season or if the plants are starved and neglected. However, some varieties show fantastic disease-resistance even when others around them succumb to fungal infection. These include some old roses, such as Gallicas and Albas, and modern Shrub roses like the Rugosas. Good resistance to disease is also found among newer varieties of English and Modern Bush rose. The roses highlighted on these pages as reliably disease-resistant are those that will remain disease-free in most situations without the need for regular spraying.

Seasonal performance

A rose marked in the directory as summer-flowering will have one main flowering period, in early to midsummer. Repeat-flowering roses usually have two main seasons – early summer and late summer into autumn – with occasional flushes of blooms in between. A few roses, described as flowering continuously, produce a display throughout the season. An indication is given where autumn hips provide further interest.

Shrub roses

Shrub roses have a less formal habit than Modern Bush roses and are used in the garden in the same way as other flowering shrubs. Most carry their flowers in a graceful manner all over the plants; some produce one prolific show of flowers in early summer, while others bloom again later in the season.

Summer-flowering Shrub roses

Summer-flowering Shrub roses are those delightful old-fashioned roses, with blooms crammed with petals, fragrance and character. Many played an important historical role in the development of modern roses (*see* pages 9–11 and 16–17), yet are still worthy of a place in today's gardens. Most produce just one magnificent display in early summer. They are generally tough and reliable, and require little attention.

Rosa × *alba* 'Alba Semiplena'
○ ○ ✿ ❖ SUMMER-FLOWERING, AUTUMN HIPS
H 2.2m (7ft) S 1.5m (5ft)

This is an upright, vigorous Alba rose with healthy, blue-green foliage. The large, barely double, delicate blooms, upward-facing and pure white with golden stamens, are carried in clusters. The fragrance is wonderful – this rose is grown for the production of Attar of Roses. Red hips follow in autumn. It is tough, disease-resistant, reliable and easy to grow in any situation.

'Belle de Crécy'
○ ✿ ❖ SUMMER-FLOWERING
H 1.5m (5ft) S 1.2m (4ft)

This is a lovely Gallica rose with arching stems, olive-green foliage and few thorns. The flattened, rosette-shaped flowers are cerise-pink with hints of mauve and very fragrant. It copes with poor growing conditions and is fairly disease-free, but can be prone to mildew.

'Cardinal de Richelieu'
✿ ❖ SUMMER-FLOWERING
H 1.5m (5ft) S 1.2m (4ft)

This Gallica rose has dark green foliage and almost thornless stems. The recurved petals make the dark purple-red, deliciously fragrant flowers almost rounded. Unlike other Gallicas, this needs fertile soil and plenty of fertilizer. Thin stems annually when pruning in winter to prevent crowded growth.

'Celsiana'
○ ✿ ❖ SUMMER-FLOWERING
H 1.8m (6ft) S 1.5m (5ft)

'Celsiana' is a lovely Damask rose, with arching stems and grey-green foliage. The blooms are large, open, semi-double and soft pink; the golden stamens have a wonderful fragrance. This beautiful rose is tough, disease-resistant, easy to grow and an ideal choice for an informal garden.

Rosa × *centifolia* 'Cristata'
✿ ❖ SUMMER-FLOWERING
H and S 1.2m (4ft)

Once called 'Chapeau de Napoléon', this Centifolia rose is known as the crested moss rose because of its curious encrusted buds, which appear to be covered in moss. They open to double, gently drooping, fragrant, pink blooms carried on arching stems. The shrub is loose in habit and might need support to show the flowers to advantage.

'Charles de Mills'
○ ❋ ❖ SUMMER-FLOWERING
H 1.5m (5ft) S 1.2m (4ft)

A vigorous Gallica rose, 'Charles de Mills' has elegant, arching growth producing glorious, large flowers of deep crimson with a rich fragrance. The blooms are flattened with many petals and are often quartered. As they age, the colour changes to purple at the edge of the petals. It has healthy foliage, is disease-resistant and is a reliable performer, even in exposed situations.

'Complicata'
�○○❋❖ SUMMER-FLOWERING
H 1.5m (5ft) S 1.8m (6ft)

Probably a hybrid between a Gallica and our native dog rose, this charming variety has large, single, scented, dog rose flowers of pure pink with golden stamens. It forms a spreading shrub, with strong stems and disease-resistant foliage. A versatile plant, it is at home on a rustic tripod, in a hedgerow, in the corner of a paddock or growing into an old apple tree. It tolerates dry soil.

Rosa gallica var. *officinalis*
�○○❋❖ SUMMER-FLOWERING
H and S 1.2m (4ft)

The apothecary's rose, also known as the Red Rose of Lancaster, is perhaps the oldest rose in cultivation and has a strong, old-rose fragrance. Semi-double, crimson blooms with golden stamens open in succession over a long period. It tolerates dry and exposed sites, forming a compact bush with upright stems and light green foliage that is very disease-resistant. It makes a good low hedge.

Rosa gallica 'Versicolor'
�○○❋❖ SUMMER-FLOWERING
H and S 1.2m (4ft)

Familiar to many as *Rosa mundi*, this is similar in size and habit to *R. gallica* var. *officinalis* (*see* above) and has the same healthy foliage and robust constitution. Semi-double, pink flowers striped crimson, with golden stamens, are striking and showy, and bloom over a long period. It is disease-resistant and tolerates poor soil conditions. This rose makes an attractive low hedge.

'Geranium'
�○○ ❖ SUMMER-FLOWERING, AUTUMN HIPS
H 2.5m (8ft) S 2.2m (7ft)

Also known as *Rosa moyesii* 'Geranium', this is a large, arching Shrub rose with attractive foliage. Bright red, single flowers are followed by long, oval hips that last well into winter. It is excellent in big gardens and naturalistic planting schemes, and good on a rustic tripod. It is disease-resistant, succeeds on any soil and is ideal for inhospitable sites where regular maintenance is difficult.

'Impératrice Joséphine'
�○○❋❖ SUMMER-FLOWERING, AUTUMN HIPS
H 1.2m (4ft) S 1m (40in)

Also known as 'Empress Joséphine', this is a compact and bushy Gallica rose with few thorns and healthy, disease-resistant foliage. Large, loose, double blooms, rose-pink suffused with deep pink, have a strong fragrance. Orange hips follow the flowers in autumn, giving another season of interest. It is a reliable rose that grows on any soil.

'Ipsilante'
◊ ○ �֎ ❖ SUMMER-FLOWERING
H 1.5m (5ft) S 1.2m (4ft)

'Ipsilante' is a vigorous Gallica rose with very disease-resistant foliage and strong stems. The blooms are large, pale pink, delightfully flattened and quartered – the very essence of a beautiful old rose, with a glorious rich fragrance. It is a reliable performer on any soil, and will withstand heavy rain and strong wind.

'Madame Hardy'
✖ ❖ SUMMER-FLOWERING
H 1.5m (5ft) S 1.2m (4ft)

This is a strong-growing, upright Damask rose with light green foliage. Pretty, winged, green buds open to pure white blooms, perfectly cupped with slightly recurved outer petals. The fragrance is fresh and lemony. This is one of the most beautiful white roses. It is mostly fairly healthy, but is best in an open position on fertile soil.

'Tuscany Superb'
◊ ○ ✖ ❖ SUMMER-FLOWERING
H 1.5m (5ft) S 1m (40in)

This Gallica rose is known as the double velvet rose, so called because of the texture of its petals. It bears sumptuous, deep-purple, fragrant blooms with wavy petals and a few golden stamens in the centre of the flowers. The blooms are weather-resistant, and the plant tolerates poor soil and is strong and bushy, with upright stems and healthy, disease-resistant foliage.

'Königin von Dänemark'
◐ ◊ ○ ✖ ❖ SUMMER-FLOWERING
H 1.5m (5ft) S 1.2m (4ft)

A tough, disease-resistant Alba rose, succeeding in almost any situation and soil, this has strong stems, an upright habit, grey-green leaves and exquisite quartered blooms of glowing pink, paler towards the edge of the flower. It has a strong old-rose fragrance. It is one of the most reliable summer-flowering roses and is excellent in a mixed border.

'Maiden's Blush'
◊ ○ ✖ ❖ SUMMER-FLOWERING
H 1.5m (5ft) S 1.2m (4ft)

This Alba rose has an upright habit with strong stems and healthy, blue-green foliage. The flowers are upward-facing, loose rosettes of blush-pink petals with a strong and delicious fragrance. It is a very hardy rose that is good in cold and wet, as well as hot and dry, situations. The disease-resistant foliage is as much an asset as the flowers.

'William Lobb'
◊ ○ ✖ ❖ SUMMER-FLOWERING
H and S 1.8m (6ft)

Known as the old velvet Moss rose, this produces mossy buds that open to very fragrant, double, dark crimson blooms, fading to mauve-grey. It is strong-growing, with disease-resistant foliage and sturdy stems, and is best at the back of a border or among other vigorous shrubs. Given support, it will scramble and climb. It grows on any soil.

Repeat-flowering Shrub roses

These roses have the charm of the old-fashioned, summer-flowering Shrub roses but they repeat flower during the summer and into autumn, some of them producing blooms almost continuously throughout the season. The group includes ancient China roses, old Bourbons, Portlands and the more recent Hybrid Musk roses (*see* pages 16–17). Most are ideal growing in mixed borders and should be considered along with any other flowering shrubs. Many repeat-flowering Shrub roses are fragrant. Some are tough and reliable, while others need cosseting.

'Bonica'
◐ ❖ REPEAT-FLOWERING, AUTUMN HIPS
H 1.2m (4ft) S 1.5m (5ft)

'Bonica' is a modern Shrub rose with a spreading, arching habit and abundant glossy green leaves. The small, double, mid-pink flowers are carried in light sprays. Blooms are freely produced throughout the summer and will develop into small orange hips if not dead-headed. It is a tough, disease-resistant rose, good for mixed borders, hedging and coastal gardens.

'Ballerina'
◐ ❖ REPEAT-FLOWERING
H and S 1.2m (4ft)

'Ballerina' is a modern Shrub rose with arching stems and dark green foliage. The flowers are small and single, very pale pink in the centre and deep pink towards the edge of the petals, with golden-yellow stamens. On mature plants they are freely carried in large sprays almost continuously throughout the summer. The blooms are slightly fragrant. This is a reliable, disease-resistant rose that is perfect for pots, a small garden and a mixed border. It is a good choice for coastal gardens.

'Blanche Double de Coubert'
◐ ✳ ❖ REPEAT-FLOWERING
H and S 1.8m (6ft)

This is a typical Rugosa rose, forming a thorny shrub with upright stems and apple-green leaves. The large, loose-petalled, double, pure white flowers are upward-facing and are deliciously fragrant. This Rugosa does not form large hips in autumn but, like other Rugosas, it is a tough, reliable rose, disease-resistant and tolerant. It makes a good impenetrable hedge. Sadly, it is rarely available but it is worth looking out for. It is sometimes sold under the name 'Blanc Double de Coubert'.

'Buff Beauty'
◑◐◯ ✳ ❖ REPEAT-FLOWERING
H and S 1.5m (5ft)

A Hybrid Musk rose with strong, spreading branches and dark green foliage, reddish at the end of the shoots, this carries large, loose clusters of double flowers with a warm, tea fragrance. The blooms are a lovely shade of soft apricot, paler at the edge of the flower where the outer petals reflex when fully open. It is reliable, disease-resistant and tolerant of some shade and dry soil. It is superb grown with blue-flowering perennials.

'Cornelia'
◐ ◯ ✿ ❖ REPEAT-FLOWERING
H and S 1.5m (5ft)

This is a lovely Hybrid Musk rose with reddish, arching stems and dark green, disease-resistant foliage. It produces abundant loose clusters of double, strawberry-pink blooms tinged with gold in the centres; the scent is strong and delicious. 'Cornelia' is a reliable performer that is excellent for a larger bed or a mixed border, makes a lovely hedge, and succeeds in partial shade.

'De Rescht'
◐ ◯ ✿ ❖ REPEAT-FLOWERING
H 1m (40in) S 75cm (30in)

A very reliable and excellent Portland rose, this makes a dense and bushy shrub with mid-green, disease-resistant foliage. The tidy, well-formed blooms are flattened, loosely quartered rosettes of crimson-purple petals held well above the foliage. They are very fragrant and are produced throughout the season. It makes a good low hedge, and tolerates some shade.

'Felicia'
◐ ◯ ✿ ❖ REPEAT-FLOWERING
H and S 1.5m (5ft)

'Felicia' is a delightful disease-resistant, shade-tolerant, Hybrid Musk rose with strong, arching stems and large, dark green leaves. The highly fragrant flowers are loosely double, pale pink, deeper in the centre. The large clusters can weigh the branches down, broadening the shrub's spread. It is a wonderful rose for a big bed or beside a wide path.

'Ferdinand Pichard'
✿ ❖ REPEAT-FLOWERING
H and S 1.2m (4ft)

An early Hybrid Perpetual rose, and probably the best repeat-flowering Shrub rose with striped flowers, this forms an upright, bushy shrub with matt green foliage. The rounded blooms have incurved petals that reflex at the edges as the flowers open; they are mauve-pink striped with crimson and purple, and very fragrant. This rose grows best in a warm, sunny position and needs regular feeding or the foliage will yellow.

'Fru Dagmar Hastrup'
◌ ◯ ❖ REPEAT-FLOWERING, AUTUMN HIPS
H and S 1.5m (5ft)

This is a reliable Rugosa rose, forming a broad shrub with light brown, very thorny stems and apple-green foliage. The flowers are single, pale pink with cream stamens, slightly fragrant and followed by large, orange-red hips. No dead-heading is needed. This rose will grow on poor soil and is extremely weather- and disease-resistant. It is also a good choice for gardens with rabbits and deer, which tend to leave it alone.

'Golden Wings'
✿ ❖ REPEAT-FLOWERING
H and S 1.5m (5ft)

'Golden Wings' is a lovely modern Shrub rose, forming an open bush with dark green leaves. The large, single flowers are golden yellow, with red-brown stamens and a fresh fragrance. This rose blooms with wonderful continuity, but needs good air circulation around it and can be disease-prone. It is good as part of a yellow scheme in a mixed border.

'Jacqueline du Pré'

◊ ◯ ❖ REPEAT-FLOWERING

H and S 90cm (3ft)

A useful modern Shrub rose of compact, bushy habit with dark green foliage, this has semi-double flowers of medium size that are white with golden stamens and a light scent. It flowers very freely and reliably. Related to *Rosa spinosissima*, it is hardy and tolerant of poor soil and weather; it is also very disease-resistant.

'Madame Isaac Pereire'

❄ ❖ REPEAT-FLOWERING

H 1.5m (5ft) S 1.2m (4ft)

This gorgeous Bourbon rose has very large, loosely double, cup-shaped, crimson-pink flowers with reflexed edges to the petals and a sweet, heavy fragrance. Its habit is arching and strong, but open when grown as a shrub; it is perhaps better on a tripod or grown as a short climber. It can be prone to mildew and black spot, but is more resistant than the widely planted Bourbon 'Zéphirine Drouhin'.

'Madame Knorr'

◐ ◊ ◯ ❄ ❖ REPEAT-FLOWERING

H 1.2m (4ft) S 90cm (3ft)

Familiar to many as 'Comte de Chambord', this compact Portland rose is ideal for a small garden. It has upright stems and light green, disease-resistant foliage. The large, quartered blooms open flat and are upward-facing; they are warm pink and deliciously scented. This is a tough rose that is easy to grow, even in dry soil, but does not like to be smothered by other plants.

'Marchesa Boccella'

◊ ❄ ❖ REPEAT-FLOWERING

H 1.2m (4ft) S 90cm (3ft)

Sometimes known as 'Jacques Cartier', this is a Portland rose making a neat plant with upright stems and light green foliage. The large blooms are rosette-shaped, loosely quartered, deep pink and very fragrant; they face upwards on the plant. It repeats well throughout the summer. As a Portland rose, it is tough, tolerates dry as well as cold, wet situations, and is usually disease-free.

Rosa × odorata 'Mutabilis'

◊ ❄ ❖ REPEAT-FLOWERING

H 2.5m (8ft) S 1.8m (6ft)

A China rose also known as *Rosa chinensis* 'Mutabilis', this is a graceful creature with slender growth and dark green leaves flushed deep red. Delicate, very fragrant, single blooms, produced with remarkable continuity, open soft creamy yellow and change to copper-orange and crimson-pink; all colours can appear in a cluster at any one time. Tolerating dry soil, it is ideal for a sunny wall and a great alternative to a climber.

Rosa × odorata 'Pallida'

❄ ❖ REPEAT-FLOWERING

H 1.2m (4ft) S 90cm (3ft)

This old China rose, also known as 'Old Blush China', is called the monthly rose because it flowers for such a long period – from mid-spring to winter. The flowers are pale pink, in dainty clusters and not particularly showy, but very fragrant. The growth is light and twiggy and can be trained against a warm wall, where you could find it in flower at any time. It is not the most exciting rose, but it has a certain charm.

'Penelope'
◐ ◯ ✿ ❖ REPEAT-FLOWERING, AUTUMN HIPS
H and S 1.8m (6ft)

'Penelope' is an underrated Hybrid Musk rose, with branching stems and dark green, disease-resistant leaves. The flowers are double, creamy pink and very fragrant. They are carried in large clusters and are freely produced through the season. 'Penelope' repeat flowers well and, if not dead-headed later in the season, produces small, coral-red hips.

'Rhapsody in Blue'
◯ ✿ ❖ REPEAT-FLOWERING
H 1.2m (4ft) S 90cm (3ft)

Often regarded as a Floribunda rose, this is a tall, open shrub with smooth stems and mid-green foliage. The loosely semi-double flowers are iridescent purple, fading to mauve-grey. They are freely produced through the season and have a strong, orange-like fragrance. Reliably repeat-flowering and disease-resistant, it is an excellent rose for a mixed border, particularly in association with grey foliage shrubs.

'Roseraie de l'Haÿ'
◊ ◯ ✿ ❖ REPEAT-FLOWERING
H and S 2.2m (7ft)

This is a large, vigorous, disease-resistant shrub of bushy habit, with thorny stems and bright green leaves. The large blooms are loosely double, wine purple, with a strong, sweet fragrance. This double-flowering Rugosa rose does not produce hips like the single varieties do. It is an excellent rose for poor growing conditions and is a good choice for either a mixed border or a wild garden.

'Rosy Cushion'
◊ ◯ ❖ REPEAT-FLOWERING
H 1.2m (4ft) S 1m (40in)

'Rosy Cushion' lives up to its name, forming a dense, bushy, rounded shrub. It has healthy, disease-resistant foliage and a continuous display of flowers from summer into autumn. The blooms are single or partially semi-double, soft pink, with a slight scent. It makes a good choice for the front of a mixed border or for a dry scree or gravel area.

Rosa rugosa 'Alba'
◊ ◯ ✿ ❖ REPEAT-FLOWERING, AUTUMN HIPS
H and S 1.8m (6ft)

A typical Rugosa rose, this is a thorny shrub with upright stems and apple-green leaves. The pure white, single flowers are large, saucer-shaped and deliciously fragrant. They are followed by big orange-red hips, which stay on the plants after the leaves have fallen. It is a tough, disease-resistant, reliable rose that is tolerant of dry soil, and is good as a hedge and in a mixed border.

'The Fairy'
❖ REPEAT-FLOWERING
H 75cm (30in) S 1m (40in)

As its name implies, this Polyantha rose is a very small shrub. It has spreading, arching growth and tiny leaves. The small, pink, pompon flowers appear in little sprays all through the season; once it gets going, it flowers continuously. The blooms are slightly fragrant. It is a tough, reliable and compact rose, ideal for a narrow border or a small garden.

Ground-cover roses

These have lax, ground-hugging stems and lots of tiny leaves. Flowers are small, usually in clusters, so they make colourful mounds on sunny banks and are lovely cascading over walls. Needing little maintenance, they can be sheared to control size and spread. Some produce colourful hips in autumn.

'Suffolk'
◐ ❖ REPEAT-FLOWERING, AUTUMN HIPS
H 45cm (18in) S 1m (40in)

This is a striking Ground-cover rose, forming a low mound with small, dark green, disease-resistant leaves. The single flowers are dark red with golden stamens, and are carried in profuse, loose clusters. They are not fragrant, but are followed by orange-red hips in autumn. It is effective trailing over low walls; the deep-red flowers work well with flint or grey stone walls.

'Flower Carpet Pink'
◊ ◐ ❖ REPEAT-FLOWERING
H 60cm (2ft) S 1.2m (4ft)

The original Flower Carpet rose forms a low, spreading mound of green stems and mid-green, shiny foliage. The small flowers are semi-double, strong pink and carried in large clusters all summer. It is disease-resistant, and works well in a pot, on a dry, sunny bank or at the front of a border; it is very effective alongside silver- or purple-leaved shrubs.

'Grouse 2000'
◊ ◐ ✽ ❖ REPEAT-FLOWERING, AUTUMN HIPS
H 60cm (2ft) S 1m (40in)

This improved, more compact, vigorous form of 'Grouse' grows close to the ground, with disease-resistant, mid-green foliage. The small, single, highly scented pink flowers are freely produced in small clusters and repeat well through the summer. Bright red hips follow. It succeeds in dry soil, so is good at the base of a wall, which it will use for support, climbing to about 90cm (3ft).

'Worcestershire'
◐ ◯ ❖ REPEAT-FLOWERING
H 60cm (2ft) S 90cm (3ft)

'Worcestershire' has disease-resistant, mid-green, glossy foliage. The semi-double flowers are clear yellow with golden stamens and are freely produced in loose clusters throughout summer and autumn. This is a good choice for ground cover in semi-shade and works well with periwinkle (*Vinca*) and *Euonymus fortunei* 'Emerald 'n' Gold'.

'Flower Carpet White'
◊ ◐ ❖ REPEAT-FLOWERING
H 60cm (2ft) S 1.2m (4ft)

This is similar in habit to 'Flower Carpet Pink' (*see* above), but has dark green foliage and pure white flowers. It flowers just as freely and continuously, but is not quite as vigorous. It is resistant to disease and tolerates dry soil. As ground cover, it works well with *Alchemilla mollis*; it is also useful in front of low, dark evergreens.

'Scented Carpet'
◐ ✽ ❖ REPEAT-FLOWERING
H 60cm (2ft) S 1m (40in)

This pretty Ground-cover rose has shiny, neat, disease-resistant foliage on arching stems. The small, single flowers, lilac-pink with white centres, are wonderfully fragrant and repeat well. It grows to form a lovely mat of flowers, particularly effective in scree or gravel.

English roses

The English roses, bred by David Austin, are modern Shrub roses with all the charm of old-fashioned roses. They are renowned for their grace, the exquisite beauty of their flowers, and their fragrance. English roses include many disease-resistant varieties that will succeed in a range of locations but excel in the mixed border with other shrubs and perennials. Some of the English roses make good climbers (*see* pages 102–5).

'Claire Austin'
❋ ❖ REPEAT-FLOWERING
H 1.2m (4ft) S 90cm (3ft)

The best of the white English roses, this forms a graceful shrub with arching branches and abundant mid-green leaves. The lemon-tinted buds open to full, cup-shaped blooms with incurved petals of pure white – reminiscent of peonies. The fragrance is complex, sweet and delicious. A strong-growing rose, it usually remains free of disease.

'Alan Titchmarsh'
◐ ❋ ❖ REPEAT-FLOWERING
H 2m (6ft) S 1.2m (4ft)

Just like its namesake, this is a tough and healthy garden subject! The stems are slightly arching and carry large, rounded buds that open to big blooms with layer upon layer of delightfully incurved petals. The petals are deep old-rose pink, the colour more intense in the heart of the flower. The blooms have a wonderful old-rose fragrance – just what you would expect from such a lovely flower. The habit improves with age and the foliage is disease-resistant.

'Charlotte'
◐ ❋ ❖ REPEAT-FLOWERING
H 90cm (3ft) S 75cm (30in)

'Charlotte' is an excellent English rose of compact, upright, bushy habit, which makes it the perfect choice for a small garden or a narrow border. The beautifully formed flowers are cup-shaped, soft yellow and deliciously Tea-rose scented. This is a healthy, disease-resistant rose that is also extremely hardy, so it is suitable for cold gardens. In addition, the short petals make this an appropriate choice for windy situations.

'Crocus Rose'
◑ ◇ ❋ ❖ REPEAT-FLOWERING
H 1.2m (4ft) S 90cm (3ft)

Although not the most widely planted of the English roses, many consider it to be one of the best. It is strong-growing, free-flowering, very reliable and will succeed in partial shade and on dry soil. The large, rosette-shaped, apricot-cream flowers become fuller and paler with age; they are cup-shaped as they open and the outer petals reflex when mature. The blooms are freely produced in clusters at the end of arching stems and are wonderfully tea-scented.

'Crown Princess Margareta'

◐ ❋ ❖ REPEAT-FLOWERING

H 1.5m (5ft) S 1.2m (4ft)

This is a tall rose that is ideal for the back of a border and can also be grown as a short climber on a pillar or obelisk. It has arching stems and dark green foliage. The blooms are many-petalled rosettes of apricot-orange petals with a fruity fragrance and are freely produced all summer. It is a strong, reliable rose that will thrive even if the growing conditions are not ideal, and is usually disease-free; it tolerates some shade.

'Darcey Bussell'

❍ ❋ ❖ REPEAT-FLOWERING

H 90cm (3ft) S 60cm (2ft)

This fine English rose forms a compact and bushy plant of rounded habit. It flowers freely and continuously all summer, producing clusters of many-petalled, rosette-shaped flowers of deep crimson with a strong, fruity fragrance. The compact habit of this rose makes it ideal for a small garden, for a narrow border, for a dedicated rose bed or for a pot. It is very disease-resistant.

'Gentle Hermione'

❋ ❖ REPEAT-FLOWERING

H 1.2m (4ft) S 90cm (3ft)

This rose lives up to its name. It forms a rounded shrub with arching stems that carry exquisitely beautiful flowers. Each bloom consists of a ring of blush-pink outer petals that frame cup-shaped, incurved petals of deeper pink, usually in a quartered arrangement. The overall effect is charming and is enhanced by the wonderful old-rose fragrance.

'Gertrude Jekyll'

◐ ❍ ❋ ❖ REPEAT-FLOWERING

H 1.2m (4ft) S 1m (40in)

Regarded as one of the most fragrant English roses, this is a must for every garden. It is a tall, strong-growing shrub with upright stems, ideal for growing at the back of the border, up a pillar or on a wall as a short climber. It is disease-resistant and succeeds in partial shade. The stems are thorny, the mid-green foliage healthy. The large, gently cupped, open blooms are rich pink, ravishingly fragrant with a strong old-rose perfume, and good for cutting.

'Golden Celebration'

◐ ❍ ❋ ❖ REPEAT-FLOWERING

H and S 1.2m (4ft)

One of the most flamboyant of all the English roses, this is a striking shrub that is also disease-resistant and tolerates partial shade. Rounded in habit, it has gently arching stems and mid-green foliage. Exceptionally large, rich golden-yellow blooms open as petal-filled cups, becoming more rounded later; the outer petals are slightly reflexed. The blooms are tea-scented and good for cutting.

'Grace'

❍ ❋ ❖ REPEAT-FLOWERING

H and S 1.2m (4ft)

'Grace' is a light, airy rose with slender, well-branched stems and apple-green leaves. The apricot flowers open cup-shaped with richly coloured centres; as the outer petals reflex and grow paler, the wonderfully tea-scented blooms become perfectly rosette-shaped. Freely produced all summer, they are reliably weather- and disease-resistant. This is an excellent rose to grow in a large terracotta pot.

'Graham Thomas'
✼ ❖ REPEAT-FLOWERING
H and S 1.2m (4ft)

Perhaps the best-known of the English roses, this has remained popular despite numerous other introductions. It is a vigorous and rather upright shrub, with mid-green foliage. Cup-shaped blooms are a clear, rich golden yellow, with a fresh, tea fragrance; good for cutting. It is best supported, maybe on an arch or arbour, as the stems can be weighed down by the heavy flower clusters.

'Jubilee Celebration'
◯ ✼ ❖ REPEAT-FLOWERING
H and S 1.2m (4ft)

An English rose with opulent, rounded blooms of rich salmon pink with golden highlights on the underside of the petals, this is a disease-resistant rose that makes a good rounded shrub. The flowers, held above the foliage, are well displayed despite the stems arching with their weight. It flowers continuously and freely, is deliciously fruit-scented and fits in any scheme of shrubs and perennials.

'Lady of Shalott'
◯ ✼ ❖ REPEAT-FLOWERING
H 1.2m (4ft) S 1m (40in)

This is a superb English rose that quickly forms a bushy, slightly arching shrub with mid-green leaves, copper when young. The blooms, upward-facing cups of incurved petals, salmon-pink on the upper side and warm orange-gold on the reverse, have a spicy tea scent and are freely produced all season. It is easy to grow, has a strong constitution and is weather- and disease-resistant.

'Harlow Carr'
◑ ◊ ◯ ✼ ❖ REPEAT-FLOWERING
H 1.2m (4ft) S 1m (40in)

It does not produce the most classically beautiful blooms, but this rose is tough, disease-resistant and reliable. It forms a rounded, well-branched shrub with flowering shoots down to ground level. The medium-sized flowers are shallow cups of pure pink with a strong, old-rose fragrance. It flowers very freely all through the season. This is a good rose for the border or as a low hedge, and tolerates dry, exposed and shady sites.

'Lady Emma Hamilton'
◯ ✼ ❖ REPEAT-FLOWERING
H 1.2m (4ft) S 1m (40in)

This is an excellent rose with strong stems and healthy, dark green leaves, enhanced by copper-coloured new shoots. The blooms are globe-shaped, red in bud opening to soft glowing, apricot orange, with a strong, fruity fragrance. Flowers are freely produced all through the season, and the foliage remains disease-free provided it is not overcrowded by neighbouring plants.

'Molineux'
◑ ◯ ✼ ❖ REPEAT-FLOWERING
H 90cm (3ft) S 60cm (2ft)

An upright, compact habit makes this an excellent rose for a small garden, narrow border, mixed bed or low hedge. The blooms are shallow cups of golden-yellow petals with a delightful tea fragrance, good for cutting and borne continually all season. It is very disease-resistant and tolerates cold conditions and partial shade. It works well with yellow-variegated evergreens.

'Munstead Wood'
○ ✿ ❖ REPEAT-FLOWERING
H 90cm (3ft) S 75cm (30in)

This English rose is a bushy, spreading shrub with mid-green foliage, bronze-red when young. The crimson buds open deep purple-crimson, paler at the edge of the outer petals that ring the shallow, cup-shaped, petal-filled centre. The luxurious, velvety blooms have a strong, fruity, old-rose fragrance. This disease-resistant variety is lovely with lavender and other silver-foliage shrubs.

'Port Sunlight'
◌ ○ ✿ ❖ REPEAT-FLOWERING
H 1.5m (5ft) S 1m (40in)

This is a reliable, weather- and disease-resistant, upright rose. The rosette-shaped blooms are warm apricot, paler at the edge of the petals. Plant it where its rich tea fragrance can be enjoyed, or at the back of a border, where its colouring would make it a fine partner for deep-blue delphiniums. It is one of the best apricot roses.

'Princess Alexandra of Kent'
○ ✿ ❖ REPEAT FLOWERING
H 1m (40in) S 75cm (30in)

This strong, healthy rose forms a neat, rounded bush with sturdy, upright stems. The foliage is deep green and disease-resistant. The blooms are upward-facing, deep cups crowded with rich pink petals, a little paler at the edge of the flowers. They have a rich tea fragrance and are long-lasting and weather-resistant. If space allows, three plants grouped together look better than a single one.

'Queen of Sweden'
◑ ◌ ○ ❖ REPEAT-FLOWERING
H 1m (40in) S 75cm (30in)

This is an upright, bushy English rose with strong stems and disease-resistant, dark green foliage. It takes up little space, so is ideal for a small garden or narrow border. The delightful cup-shaped blooms are soft apricot pink fading to pale pink; they are only lightly scented, but are freely produced and weather-resistant. It is a lovely rose for the front of a mixed border, for a rose bed, for hedging or for pots.

'Rosemoor'
◑ ◌ ○ ✿ ❖ REPEAT-FLOWERING
H 1m (40in) S 75cm (30in)

A bushy rose with mid-green, disease-resistant foliage, this bears abundant pale pink, rosette-shaped blooms all summer. They have a strong fragrance. The outer petals reflex a little as the flowers mature, and small green eyes develop in the centres. A versatile rose, it mixes well with perennials and other shrubs and makes a good low hedge; it tolerates partial shade and dry soil.

'Scepter'd Isle'
✿ ❖ REPEAT-FLOWERING
H 90cm (3ft) S 75cm (30in)

This lovely upright rose carries its flowers well above the foliage. The blooms are double cups with incurved petals, but when fully open the stamens in the middle are revealed. The petals are pink, paler towards the outside of the flower, and the scent is strong and powerful. It is a free-flowering variety that blooms continuously through the season. It can be pruned very lightly to make a taller shrub suitable for the back of a border.

'Freedom'
❖ REPEAT-FLOWERING

H 75cm (30in) S 60cm (2ft)

A strong, bushy rose, 'Freedom' has glossy, medium-sized leaves that are red when young. The blooms, freely produced throughout the summer and early autumn, are rich golden yellow, with spiralled petals in the centre of the bloom and a slight fragrance. It is an excellent bedding rose that is fairly disease-resistant and free-flowering.

'Julia's Rose'
❖ REPEAT-FLOWERING

H 1m (40in) S 60cm (2ft)

This unusual Hybrid Tea rose, with slender upright growth, can be grown as a shrub if lightly pruned. Elegantly pointed buds open to rounded blooms in shades of coffee, copper and pink – colouring that makes it popular with flower arrangers. It has a reputation for being tricky to grow; on wet soil try it in a pot. Watch out for disease.

'King's Macc'
✿ ❖ REPEAT-FLOWERING

H 90cm (3ft) S 75cm (30in)

A splendid rose with large, mid-green leaves, 'King's Macc' bears classically shaped blooms that open from spiralled buds in a blend of apricot, cream and copper, with hints of golden yellow. The large blooms are strongly scented. This rose is ideal for cutting, and looks good in a rose bed or a mixed border.

'Grandpa Dickson'
❖ REPEAT-FLOWERING

H 75cm (30in) S 60cm (2ft)

'Grandpa Dickson' is a short, upright rose with large, dark green leaves. The big blooms are pale yellow and slightly fragrant. The outer petals sometimes have a pink tinge to them in bright, sunny weather. It repeat flowers well during the season and is a good bedding rose. This variety has remained popular for many years, despite its unremarkable colour.

'Just Joey'
✿ ❖ REPEAT-FLOWERING

H 90cm (3ft) S 75cm (30in)

This is a much-loved rose, with an open growth habit and dark green leaves that are red when young. The delightful blooms have delicately waved petals of rich, copper-orange; although not densely packed with petals, they have a charm and lightness, and a good scent. It flowers freely throughout the season and is excellent for cutting and as a bedding rose.

'Mrs Oakley Fisher'
❖ REPEAT-FLOWERING

H 75cm (30in) S 60cm (2ft)

Not often seen, this is a delicate rose with slender, upright stems and dark green, purple-flushed leaves. The blooms are single, with gently waved petals of rich apricot and a subtle fragrance. This is a good rose for a mixed border provided it does not have too much competition from its neighbours. It can be grown as a taller shrub, up to 1.5m (5ft), if pruned lightly.

'Pascali'
○ ❖ REPEAT-FLOWERING
H 1m (40in) S 75cm (30in)

'Pascali' is a strong, disease-resistant rose with attractive mid-green foliage. The beautifully formed, creamy-white flowers are carried on strong stems and have a light fragrance. It has long been regarded as the best white Hybrid Tea, good for exhibiting and cutting. Like all white roses, the edges of the blooms can blush as they age in strong sunlight.

'Paul Shirville'
✳ ❖ REPEAT-FLOWERING
H 1m (40in) S 75cm (30in)

This rose forms a vigorous bush with glossy, dark green foliage. Elegant, pointed buds open to perfectly formed blooms with high centres. They have a lovely fragrance, and the gently waved petals are shades of salmon pink, deeper towards the edge. It is an excellent bedding rose that repeat flowers well throughout the season.

'Peace'
◊ ❖ REPEAT-FLOWERING
H 1.2m (4ft) S 1m (40in)

A sizeable, vigorous, open bush with big green, glossy leaves, this rose produces exceptionally large blooms of pale yellow, flushed pink at the edge of the petals. Although not particularly elegant in bud, they are at their most attractive when fully open, and have a light fragrance. 'Peace' can be grown as a shrub and competes well in a mixed border. It is a tough rose, performing on poor soil and even when neglected.

'Remember Me'
❖ REPEAT-FLOWERING
H and S 75cm (30in)

This is a bushy rose with large, mid-green leaves. The deep-copper blooms can appear singly, but are often carried in small clusters; they have a light fragrance. This repeats well and is a good bedding rose. The name makes it a popular choice as a memorial rose.

'Royal William'
○ ✳ ❖ REPEAT-FLOWERING
H 1.2m (4ft) S 75cm (30in)

'Royal William' is a strong, healthy, disease- and weather-resistant rose with large, dark green leaves. The exquisite flowers are rich crimson-red and are carried on strong stems. They have a light scent. This is a deservedly popular, reliable bedding rose for larger beds and is good for cutting.

'Savoy Hotel'
○ ❖ REPEAT-FLOWERING
H 1m (40in) S 60cm (2ft)

'Savoy Hotel' is a bushy rose with dark green foliage. The flowers are beautifully formed, with elegantly recurved outer petals, soft pink and deeper in the heart of the blooms, but the fragrance is slight, which is disappointing for such a stunning rose. It is free-flowering and disease-resistant, so it makes a good bedding rose; it is also good for cutting.

'Silver Jubilee'
❂ ✻ ❖ REPEAT-FLOWERING
H and S 75cm (30in)

'Silver Jubilee' is a strong-growing rose with plenty of healthy, dark green foliage. The superb blooms have high centres and elegantly recurved petals of pink, flushed with apricot and creamy gold, deeper into the base of the petals. This rose is fragrant, free-flowering, disease-resistant and regarded as one of the best Hybrid Tea roses.

'Tequila Sunrise'
❖ REPEAT-FLOWERING
H 75cm (30in) S 60cm (2ft)

This is a bushy rose, with glossy, mid-green foliage. The blooms open from elegantly pointed buds. They are yellow, softly edged with red, and are lightly fragrant. It repeat flowers well during the course of the season. The overall effect is very showy, making this a good choice for a strongly coloured bedding scheme.

'Velvet Fragrance'
✻ ❖ REPEAT-FLOWERING
H 1.5m (5ft) S 75cm (30in)

Unfortunately, this is a very tall rose with a rather ungainly habit. However, the blooms live up to the name: large, high-centred, with velvety crimson petals and a strong, delicious fragrance. The leaves are dark green. It is fabulous for cutting and showing, and for every gardener who wants the iconic rose bloom it is the rose to grow.

'Simply the Best'
◑ ❂ ✻ ❖ REPEAT-FLOWERING
H 1m (40in) S 75cm (30in)

'Simply the Best' is a robust, vigorous, disease-resistant variety that will succeed in partial shade. The blooms open warm orange and fade to soft apricot; they are beautifully formed and wonderfully fragrant. The flowers last well, so are good for cutting. The foliage is glossy, bright green and red when young.

'Valencia'
✻ ❖ REPEAT-FLOWERING
H 1m (40in) S 60cm (2ft)

'Valencia' is a strong-grower with bronze-green foliage. The blooms are large, cupped with a spiralled centre, in a lovely shade of light copper, and are deliciously scented. This is a good variety for cutting, and its upright habit suits a narrow border.

'Warm Wishes'
❂ ✻ ❖ REPEAT-FLOWERING
H and S 75cm (30in)

'Warm Wishes' is a strong-growing, disease-resistant, bushy rose with mid-green foliage. The large, high-centred, beautifully formed blooms are soft apricot pink with wonderful shading in the petals. The fragrance is rich and delightful. It repeat flowers reliably and remains healthy through the season. It has won many well-deserved awards.

Floribunda roses

Floribunda roses are also known as Cluster-flowered bush roses because they carry their blooms in loose clusters, rather than individually. They are known for their bright colours, their freedom of flowering and their ease of cultivation. Generally, they are less fussy than Hybrid Tea roses, but they still need feeding and pruning, and watering in dry weather. Few Floribundas are as fragrant as Hybrid Teas, but they make up for it by contributing lots of colour throughout the season.

'Absolutely Fabulous'
◐ ◯ ✻ ❖ REPEAT-FLOWERING
H 75cm (30in) S 60cm (2ft)

A compact rose of wonderfully even growth habit, with plenty of shining foliage, this is an outstanding variety. The many-petalled blooms have ruffled petals of warm, butter yellow and are carried in abundant clusters. They have a nice perfume with a hint of liquorice. It is an excellent, disease-resistant rose, good for planting in groups or in containers, and succeeds in semi-shade.

'Amber Queen'
❖ REPEAT-FLOWERING
H and S 75cm (30in)

'Amber Queen' is a low, bushy rose with abundant, dark green foliage. The large, cup-shaped, loosely double blooms are a glorious shade of amber and are carried in loose clusters. It repeat flowers well throughout the season. It has a light fragrance and is a good choice for small beds and containers.

'Arthur Bell'
◐ ✻ ❖ REPEAT-FLOWERING
H 1m (40in) S 60cm (2ft)

A tall Floribunda with upright stems and mid-green foliage, 'Arthur Bell' produces large, semi-double blooms with slightly recurved petals when fully open. The blooms open bright yellow and fade to creamy yellow, and have a strong fragrance. This is a reliable variety, even in semi-shade, and is suitable for larger beds and borders.

'Blue for You'
✻ ❖ REPEAT-FLOWERING
H 1m (40in) S 60cm (2ft)

A Floribunda of medium height, this rose has mid-green, slightly glossy foliage that remains fairly healthy all season. Semi-double blooms open mauve-purple and fade to grey-blue. The fragrance is strong, sweet and a bit like violets. This is a lovely rose for a sunny, mixed border of pastel shades.

'Brave Heart'
◯ ✻ ❖ REPEAT-FLOWERING
H 1m (40in) S 60cm (2ft)

This is an excellent Floribunda rose, also known as 'Gordon's College'. It has upright growth and healthy, dark green, glossy foliage that is red when young. The highly fragrant blooms are Hybrid Tea-shaped, with high-centred buds and scrolled petals in a lovely shade of deep coral pink. This is a disease-resistant and reliable rose that repeat flowers well.

'Champagne Moments'

◐ ❖ REPEAT-FLOWERING

H 1.2m (4ft) S 75cm (30in)

This is a lovely rose with a bushy,
shrub-like habit and glossy green leaves.
The buds are rather Hybrid Tea-shaped
and a lovely shade of apricot, opening
to many-petalled cups of rich cream;
they are lightly fragrant. It is a healthy,
disease-resistant rose that repeat flowers
well and looks good in a mixed border.

'Escapade'

◐ ✳ ❖ REPEAT-FLOWERING

H 1.2m (4ft) S 75cm (30in)

The lovely single flowers of 'Escapade'
are a beautiful shade of rosy violet, with
golden stamens, and resemble the
blooms of the dog rose (*Rosa canina*).
They are carried in loose clusters, and
are freely produced and very fragrant.
This rose has vigorous, disease-resistant,
Shrub rose-like growth and is an
excellent choice for a mixed border,
particularly in an informal garden.

'Evelyn Fison'

◐ ❖ REPEAT-FLOWERING

H and S 75cm (30in)

'Evelyn Fison' is one of the brightest,
showiest Floribundas, with compact
growth and dark green, shiny foliage,
red at the tips of the shoots. The blooms
are bright scarlet, loosely double, open
cups, and carried in large clusters. The
whole effect of the plant is striking, and
it is a reliable, disease-resistant variety
that is good for bedding.

'Fragrant Delight'

◐ ✳ ❖ REPEAT-FLOWERING

H 1m (40in) S 75cm (30in)

This makes a tidy, well-branched plant
with dark green foliage that is red when
young. The attractive buds open to
loosely double, wonderfully fragrant
blooms of salmon orange. 'Fragrant
Delight' is a disease-resistant Floribunda
that also stands up well to heavy rain.
It makes an excellent choice for any
planting scheme where a rose of
vibrant colour is required.

'Golden Wedding'

◑ ❖ REPEAT-FLOWERING

H 1m (40in) S 75cm (30in)

Unlike many so-called celebration roses,
this Floribunda is an excellent variety.
It forms a compact plant with plenty
of shiny green foliage. The sizeable,
golden-yellow, loosely double blooms
open to cups with recurved petals
revealing golden stamens. They are
carried in large clusters and are freely
produced, but have only a light scent.
This rose will succeed in partial shade.

'Help for Heroes'

◐ ✳ ❖ REPEAT-FLOWERING

H 75cm (30in) S 60cm (2ft)

'Help for Heroes' has a strong, bushy
habit and glossy, dark green, disease-
resistant leaves. It bears a mass of
fragrant, deep-red, full-petalled flowers
in abundant clusters throughout the
season, and is ideal for large containers
and mixed borders. This variety is sold
to support the Help for Heroes charity.

'Iceberg'
❖ REPEAT-FLOWERING

H 1.2m (4ft) S 1m (40in)

'Iceberg' is deservedly one of the most popular modern roses. It is a bushy plant with glossy, apple-green foliage and can be lightly pruned to form a bigger shrub. It is useful for hedging. Large, loose clusters of pure white, loosely double blooms open from scrolled, pointed buds. The petals tinge pink on the edges in sunny weather. It flowers continuously and freely and has a light fragrance.

'Korresia'
◑ ◯ ❖ REPEAT-FLOWERING

H and S 75cm (30in)

Regarded as one of the best yellow Floribundas, 'Korresia' is a compact plant with glossy, mid-green foliage. The buds are Hybrid Tea-shaped, opening to loosely double cups of pure yellow with a light, spicy fragrance. This rose repeat flowers well, is disease-resistant and blooms quite well in semi-shade.

'L'Aimant'
◯ ✳ ❖ REPEAT-FLOWERING

H 1m (40in) S 60cm (2ft)

This is an excellent Floribunda rose with strong stems and healthy, mid-green foliage. The blooms are very fragrant, double and cup-shaped, with gently rolled back and waved petals of glowing coral pink. 'L'Aimant' repeat flowers well, is disease-resistant and is a good choice for a dedicated rose bed.

'Lucky'
◯ ✳ ❖ REPEAT-FLOWERING

H 90cm (3ft) S 75cm (30in)

This excellent rose has disease-resistant, mid-green foliage. The buds are Hybrid Tea-shaped with high, scrolled centres opening to cup-shaped, fragrant blooms of clear, strong pink. They are carried in upward-facing clusters repeatedly through the season. It is a very good choice for a rose bed or a mixed border.

'Margaret Merril'
✳ ❖ REPEAT-FLOWERING

H 75cm (30in) S 60cm (2ft)

One of the loveliest pale-coloured Floribundas, 'Margaret Merril' makes a compact plant with dark green foliage. The pointed, ivory-pink buds open to cup-shaped, loosely double blooms, revealing golden stamens in the centres of the flowers. The petals are a warm ivory white with a hint of shell pink; they are deliciously scented. This is a pretty rose for any situation, including a pot.

'Pretty Lady'
◯ ✳ ❖ REPEAT-FLOWERING

H 1m (40in) S 60cm (2ft)

This is an excellent, healthy, bushy Floribunda rose of medium height with dark green foliage. The blooms are double, soft creamy peach-pink with a hint of clear pink in the petals and are wonderfully fragrant. They are carried both singly and in small clusters throughout the season. It is altogether an easy rose to grow, in the ground or in a pot, and is disease-resistant.

'Queen Elizabeth'
◑◊◯ ❖ REPEAT-FLOWERING
H 1.8m (6ft) S 75cm (30in)

'Queen Elizabeth' is an exceptionally tall, tough and disease-resistant rose, growing into an upright plant with big, glossy, dark green leaves. The large blooms are globe-shaped, with clear pink petals, and are carried in upright clusters on strong stems. The flowers are not particularly fragrant but are weather-resistant. This is a good choice for the back of a border, for poor soil and any situation where other roses fail.

'Sexy Rexy'
◯ ❖ REPEAT-FLOWERING
H 1m (40in) S 60cm (2ft)

The name accounts for some of the popularity of this Floribunda! It forms a compact, bushy plant with disease-resistant, mid-green foliage, red when young. The blooms are full-petalled, rosette-shaped in a lovely shade of soft pink, freely produced in large clusters throughout the season and lightly fragrant. This is a good bedding rose.

'Sunset Boulevard'
◯ ❖ REPEAT-FLOWERING
H 75cm (30in) S 60cm (2ft)

This is a strong-growing Floribunda with big, dark green, glossy leaves. The blooms are large, opening from Hybrid Tea-shaped buds to double blooms of glowing salmon orange. They are freely produced all through the season, but have little fragrance. This is a particularly disease-resistant rose and an ideal choice for a vibrant colour scheme.

'Tatton'
◯ ✳ ❖ REPEAT-FLOWERING
H 1m (40in) S 75cm (30in)

'Tatton' is an exceptional rose with strong growth and large, dark green, glossy leaves. The blooms are fully double, freely produced and delightfully fragrant. The petals are a blend of burnt and soft orange, and have attractive darker markings at the edges. This is an outstanding rose and a good choice for a bed dedicated to Floribundas. It is a very disease-resistant variety.

'Trumpeter'
◯ ❖ REPEAT-FLOWERING
H and S 60cm (2ft)

'Trumpeter' is an extremely compact and healthy Floribunda with mid-green leaves, red at the tips of the shoots. The double flowers open from nicely formed buds; the petals are bright, clear red and have a light fragrance. This rose blooms continuously throughout the season and usually remains healthy.

'Valentine Heart'
✳ ❖ REPEAT-FLOWERING
H 1m (40in) S 60cm (2ft)

This is one of the loveliest Floribundas. It grows well and has deep-green foliage, red-purple when young. The blooms are loosely double with frilly petals of lilac-pink, cream in the heart of the flowers. When fully open, the petals reflex to reveal golden stamens in the centre of the flower. It blooms freely all through the season and has a delightful scent.

Patio roses

Popular for their compact habit, prolific flowering and ease of cultivation, Patio roses resemble Floribundas in producing clusters of brightly coloured flowers. They are ideal for small gardens, narrow borders and pots, and are generally more robust and reliable than Miniature roses (*see* page 21).

'Sweet Dream'
❖ REPEAT-FLOWERING
H and S 45cm (18in)

'Sweet Dream' is probably the most popular Patio rose. It has an upright, bushy habit and dark green, shiny foliage. The blooms are carried in large clusters. They are shallow, open cups filled with pale, peachy-orange petals in a neat, layered arrangement. It is a reliable variety, ideal for containers, and repeat flowers throughout the season.

'Bright Smile'
◑ ❖ REPEAT-FLOWERING
H 45cm (18in) S 60cm (2ft)

This is a compact, bushy Patio rose with plenty of deep-green, shiny foliage. The semi-double blooms are clear yellow and open from pointed buds to reveal golden stamens. It is a good choice for a pot in a semi-shaded situation.

'Peter Pan'
❖ REPEAT-FLOWERING
H and S 30cm (12in)

A very compact variety, 'Peter Pan' fits into the smallest space in the garden. It is a very reliable rose with tiny, dark green, glossy leaves. The blooms are Hybrid Tea-shaped, carried in clusters, and dark red.

'Greenall's Glory'
❖ REPEAT-FLOWERING
H 45cm (18in) S 60cm (2ft)

'Greenall's Glory' is a strong-growing, slightly spreading rose with pleasing, bronze-tinted leaves. The blooms are like tiny pink Hybrid Tea roses in bud, opening to silvery-pink blooms, pink in the centre. The light flower clusters show up well against the foliage.

'Queen Mother'
✿ ❖ REPEAT-FLOWERING
H and S 45cm (18in)

This is an excellent variety, forming a spreading, rounded shrub of well-branched growth with glossy, dark green leaves. The semi-double, soft-pink flowers are freely produced throughout the season, and are unusually fragrant for a Patio rose. A good choice for a pot.

'Wildfire'
❖ REPEAT-FLOWERING
H 60cm (2ft) S 45cm (18in)

This is a compact, densely branched rose with small, matt green leaves. The blooms are bright orange, double, and open from Hybrid Tea-shaped buds; they are lightly fragrant and freely produced throughout the season.

Climbing and Rambler roses

These roses produce long stems that need support. They can be grown on walls, fences, pillars, obelisks and other structures, and the most vigorous types can be grown into trees and over buildings. Climbing and Rambler roses are similar but differ in a number of ways (*see* page 22).

Climbing roses

Climbing roses are often forms of Shrub or Modern Bush roses that have a climbing habit. They generally produce large flowers, either singly or in clusters, and most repeat flower through the season. They are good for walls, doorways, arches and restricted spaces.

'Alister Stella Gray'
✿ ❖ SUMMER-FLOWERING
H 5m (16ft) S 3m (10ft)

This is a strong-growing Climbing rose with arching stems and light green, shiny foliage. The blooms are carried in sprays. They are flattened, muddled rosettes of rich cream and are deliciously fragrant. Although this rose repeat blooms through the season, the early flush is the most prolific. It can be prone to mildew, so keep the soil moist.

'Cécile Brünner'
◐ ❖ SUMMER-FLOWERING
H 5m (16ft) S 3m (10ft)

'Cécile Brünner' is very vigorous and is ideal for high walls. The smooth, reddish stems carry dark green, pointed leaves, often with a reddish tint. The delicate, pale pink blooms are like tiny Hybrid Tea roses, pointed in bud, perfectly formed and scrolled when open. This rose performs well in semi-shade, but has only one long flowering period.

'A Shropshire Lad'
⬡ ✿ ❖ REPEAT-FLOWERING
H 3m (10ft) S 1.2m (4ft)

This is an excellent English rose that is wonderful for growing on an obelisk or arch or around a doorway. It has strong, thornless stems and disease-resistant foliage. The blooms are cup-shaped rosettes of peach-pink petals, richer in colour in the centre. They have a delicious fruity fragrance and are borne throughout the season. A tough, reliable rose, it will produce flowering shoots from the ground to the top of the plant.

'Altissimo'
❖ REPEAT-FLOWERING
H 2.5m (8ft) S 1.2m (4ft)

This is a strong, upright Climbing rose with mid-green foliage; it can also be grown as a Shrub rose. The large, single flowers are perfectly formed and are clear scarlet shaded with deeper red. Golden stamens fill the centre of each long-lasting bloom. This is a reliable variety that repeats well and is a good choice where bright colour is required.

'Compassion'
✿ ❖ REPEAT-FLOWERING
H 3m (10ft) S 1.2m (4ft)

This has always been a favourite, for its big fragrant blooms and its reliability. The stiff, upright stems carry plenty of dark green, glossy foliage. The flowers are large, Hybrid Tea-shaped and showy when fully open. The petals are salmon pink with a hint of orange and are sweetly fragrant. This rose repeat flowers well, and generally remains healthy.

'Crimson Glory'

✳️ ❖ SUMMER-FLOWERING
H 5m (16ft) S 2.5m (8ft)

This is a tall form of a climbing Hybrid Tea rose, with shiny, mid-green foliage. The large blooms are rich crimson and cup-shaped, loosely filled with velvety petals. They are deliciously fragrant and freely produced in early summer; just a few flowers appear later in the season. This is a good choice for a high, white wall or as a tall pillar rose.

'Étoile de Hollande'

✳️ ❖ REPEAT-FLOWERING
H 6m (20ft) S 3m (10ft)

This is a climbing form of a well-known Hybrid Tea rose and grows vigorously to a considerable height. The leaves are large and dark green. The blooms are deep crimson, velvety and loosely filled with soft petals; they are richly fragrant: everything a beautiful red rose should be, in fact. It produces a good crop of flowers in early summer and blooms again in early autumn. It is a lovely choice for an old stone wall.

'Golden Gate'

◯ ✳️ ❖ REPEAT-FLOWERING
H 2.5m (8ft) S 1.2m (4ft)

'Golden Gate' is short and upright, with mid-green, disease-resistant foliage. The blooms are semi-double and very loosely cupped, with slightly incurved petals. They are pure, clear yellow with golden stamens and fragrant. This rose repeat flowers well through the season and is a good choice for a pot, pillar, arch or low wall.

'Golden Showers'

◑ ❖ REPEAT-FLOWERING
H 3m (10ft) S 1.2m (4ft)

'Golden Showers' has been around for a few years, but remains as popular as ever. It has an upright habit, dark purple-tinged stems and dark green leaves; the leaves are sometimes rather sparse. The large blooms are semi-double, loosely petalled and soft yellow, fading to creamy yellow in a sunny position. They have a light fragrance and are produced with wonderful continuity. This is still one of the best Climbing roses for a shady wall.

'Iceberg'

❖ REPEAT-FLOWERING
H 3m (10ft) S 1.2m (4ft)

'Iceberg' makes an excellent Climbing rose, regarded by many as superior to the bushy Floribunda form. It has light green stems and foliage; the leaves are narrower and more pointed than those of many roses. The loosely double flowers are carried in clusters repeatedly through the season. The pure white, lightly scented petals often blush pink in hot weather. It is ideal for a pergola.

'James Galway'

✳️ ❖ REPEAT-FLOWERING
H 2.5m (8ft) S 1.2m (4ft)

'James Galway' is an English rose with strong, thornless stems that quickly reach their ultimate height. The foliage is mid-green and healthy. The flowers are large and tightly packed with layers of petals, pale pink at the edge of the bloom and rich pink in the heart of the flower. They have a strong old-rose fragrance and last well. This is a good choice for those wanting quick results and plenty of flowers.

'Lady Hillingdon'
◐ ❋ ❖ REPEAT-FLOWERING
H 5m (16ft) S 2.5m (8ft)

This is a vigorous Climbing Tea rose with lush, dark green foliage. Opening from long, pointed buds, the loose-petalled, apricot-yellow blooms tend to hang on slender stems, and are produced freely all summer and into autumn. They have a strong Tea-rose fragrance. This is a hardy rose, tolerating poor, dry soil, but grows best on a sunny, warm wall.

'Madame Alfred Carrière'
◐ ◐ ◯ ❋ ❖ REPEAT-FLOWERING
H and S 6m (20ft)

This is one of the loveliest white roses, and certainly one of the best Climbing roses. Upright and vigorous in habit, it needs a high wall or pergola to be seen at its best. Stems and foliage are light to mid-green. The cup-shaped blooms, ivory white with a hint of shell pink and fragrant, are produced freely. Hardy, disease-resistant and reliable, it tolerates dry and wet soil and some shade.

'Maigold'
◐ ◯ ❋ ❖ SUMMER-FLOWERING
H 4m (13ft) S 3m (10ft)

'Maigold' is a vigorous Climbing rose with thorny stems and glossy foliage. Its semi-double blooms open wide to reveal golden stamens. The petals are copper-gold and strongly scented. Blooms are freely produced in early summer, and a few appear later in the season. This is a reliable, tough, disease-resistant rose that succeeds in partial shade.

'Mortimer Sackler'
◯ ❋ ❖ REPEAT-FLOWERING
H 3m (10ft) S 2m (6ft)

This is a superb English rose with slender dark stems and elegantly pointed foliage. It is virtually thornless, so is ideal for an arch or doorway. The pink blooms are loose-petalled and delicate, revealing golden stamens when open. They are carried in loose clusters of a few flowers, and have a delicious old-rose fragrance. The whole effect is gentle and charming, and suits an informal garden. It is an extremely healthy, disease-resistant rose.

'New Dawn'
◐ ◯ ❋ ❖ REPEAT-FLOWERING
H 3m (10ft) S 2.5m (8ft)

One of the most popular Climbing roses, this has arching stems and healthy, shiny emerald-green foliage. Blooms are Hybrid Tea-shaped, of medium size, pale pink on the outside, deeper pink within, with a hint of salmon. They are carried in clusters and have a fresh, fruity fragrance. This is ideal for a tripod, arch, doorway or low wall. It tolerates some shade and has good disease-resistance.

'Ophelia'
❋ ❖ REPEAT-FLOWERING
H 4m (13ft) S 3m (10ft)

This is the climbing form of an old Hybrid Tea rose of great beauty. The growth habit is light, with mid-green foliage. The buds are elegant, spiralled and pointed, and open to classic Hybrid Tea blooms of palest pink. The flowers are deliciously fragrant, freely produced throughout the season and good for cutting. For best results, feed well and water regularly if the soil is dry.

'Pink Perpétué'
❖ REPEAT-FLOWERING

H 5m (16ft) S 2.5m (8ft)

This is a popular Climbing rose of vigorous habit, with mid-green foliage. The open, loosely double blooms are carried in open clusters. They are bright rose-pink and have a light fragrance. This rose repeat flowers well and is ideal grown on a pillar or a narrow wall.

'The Generous Gardener'
◐ ❉ ❖ REPEAT-FLOWERING, AUTUMN HIPS

H 3m (10ft) S 2m (6ft)

This is a strong-growing, disease-resistant English rose with dark green leaves that stay on the plant until late in the season. The blooms are double, but when fully open reveal golden stamens. The petals are warm pink in the centre of the flower, paler on the outside, and have a delicious and complex fragrance. If it is not dead-headed, this rose will produce orange hips in autumn.

'The Prince's Trust'
◐ ❖ REPEAT-FLOWERING

H 3m (10ft) S 2m (6ft)

'The Prince's Trust' is a healthy, disease-resistant and strong-growing Climbing rose with glossy, dark green foliage. The lightly fragrant, cherry-red blooms are carried in loose clusters repeatedly during the season. This is a good choice for growing on an arch, an obelisk, a wall or in a pot.

'Teasing Georgia'
◐ ◑ ❉ ❖ REPEAT-FLOWERING

H 2.5m (8ft) S 1.2m (4ft)

'Teasing Georgia' is a glorious yellow English rose of robust constitution and healthy foliage. The large blooms are open cups of deep yellow, paler at the edges, with a Tea-rose fragrance. The rose repeat flowers well over the season. This is a very hardy, disease-resistant rose that performs well in partial shade, whatever the season.

'The Pilgrim'
◑ ◐ ❉ ❖ REPEAT-FLOWERING

H 2.5m (8ft) S 1.2m (4ft)

A fast-growing rose, 'The Pilgrim' soon makes an impact in any situation. It grows well in sun or semi-shade and its emerald-green leaves are disease-resistant. The large blooms are often quartered, full of petals and clear yellow, paler at the edges. Produced right from ground level, they are deliciously scented and good for cutting. This makes an excellent pillar rose.

'Warm Welcome'
❖ REPEAT-FLOWERING

H 2m (6ft) S 60cm (2ft)

'Warm Welcome' is a Patio Climbing rose with red-purple stems and purple-tinted, dark green, slender leaves. The glowing orange flowers are semi-double, with hints of gold at the base of the petals, produced freely and continuously all through the season. A versatile Climbing rose, it is ideal for a narrow border, a wall, a container or growing up a pillar.

Rambler roses

Rambler roses produce vigorous, arching shoots that emerge from the base of the plants and have the ability to climb through or scramble over any support. They usually produce numerous small flowers, carried in sprays, in early to midsummer. Most do not repeat flower, but make up for it with the great mass of blooms they produce in the main flush. Rambler roses are tough, reliable plants that succeed in most situations and most are healthy and disease-resistant.

'Adélaïde d'Orléans'

SUMMER-FLOWERING

H 5m (16ft) S 3m (10ft)

This is a healthy, disease-resistant Rambler, with fine stems and almost evergreen foliage. The flowers are pink in bud, opening to creamy-pink, semi-double blooms. These hang on delicate stems in large clusters and are lightly but sweetly scented. The lax habit of this Rambler makes it a good choice for arches, arbours and pergolas.

'Albéric Barbier'

REPEAT-FLOWERING

H 8m (26ft) S 4m (13ft)

This lovely Rambler has vigorous green shoots and shiny, mid-green foliage, which is disease-resistant and almost evergreen. The flowers are loosely double, 10cm (4in) across, and a rich cream with a fruity fragrance. They are carried in small clusters in early summer; some re-appear later on. This rose can be grown over an outbuilding, on a high wall, or as a colonnade. It makes a good weeping standard and tolerates shade.

'Albertine'

SUMMER-FLOWERING

H 6m (20ft) S 3m (10ft)

An old favourite, 'Albertine' has red-green, arching stems and dark green leaves. The blooms open from pointed, salmon-pink buds to loosely double blooms, carried in small clusters of a few flowers. The petals are coppery pink. It is a free-flowering, very fragrant rose, but does not repeat. Grow it on a wall or a tripod, as a large shrub, or, in a wide bed, try training the stems over hoops.

'Alexandre Girault'

REPEAT-FLOWERING

H 6m (20ft) S 5m (16ft)

A vigorous Rambler with glossy green, disease-resistant foliage, this carries fragrant, crimson-pink, loosely double, quartered blooms in clusters in summer and again in autumn. This strikingly coloured rose is at its best in a purple-leaved tree such as a *Prunus*.

'American Pillar'

SUMMER-FLOWERING, AUTUMN HIPS

H 4m (13ft) S 3m (10ft)

This is a vigorous, tough, reliable rose, with strong stems and shiny, dark green foliage. Single flowers, cerise-pink with white centres and golden stamens, are produced freely in abundant clusters in midsummer, sometimes followed by dark red hips. It is a good choice to grow into an old apple tree or a purple-leaved crab (*Malus*). However, the rose can be prone to mildew later in the season.

Rosa banksiae 'Lutea'
🌢 ❊ ❖ SUMMER-FLOWERING
H 10m (33ft) S 6m (20ft)

The Banksian rose is the earliest Rambler to flower. It has fine, trailing, thornless stems and small, light green leaves. The tiny, very double flowers, creamy yellow and sweetly fragrant, are carried in posy-like clusters in late spring and early summer. This is a vigorous rose, lovely in a tree or cascading over a high wall with purple wisteria. Succeeding in dry soil, it is at its best in a warm, sunny situation.

'Bobbie James'
❊ ❖ SUMMER-FLOWERING, AUTUMN HIPS
H 10m (33ft) S 5m (16ft)

'Bobbie James' is one of the biggest and showiest Ramblers. It has bright, light green foliage and strong, thick stems that throw themselves into trees or over pergolas. In early summer they carry extravagant sprays of sweetly scented, semi-double, cream flowers with golden stamens. Each bloom is around 4cm (1¾in) across, and the sprays of flowers can be 60cm (2ft) or more across. Small orange hips follow in autumn.

'Crimson Shower'
❖ REPEAT-FLOWERING
H 5m (16ft) S 3m (10ft)

'Crimson Shower' has graceful, arching branches and shiny, dark green foliage. The loosely double, bright crimson blooms are carried in loose clusters. It flowers with great continuity from midsummer to autumn – the ideal red rose for an arch, pergola or small tree.

'Félicité Perpétué'
◑ 🌢 ◐ ❊ ❖ SUMMER-FLOWERING
H 5m (16ft) S 3m (10ft)

This is one of the finest Ramblers, with graceful, red-green stems and neat, almost evergreen, disease-resistant foliage. The scented, flattened, pompon flowers are cream to pale pink, packed with layers of petals, and hang in loose clusters in midsummer. This is a totally reliable, easy-to-grow Rambler, needing little maintenance and thriving on poor soils and in shady sites. It is lovely choice for a colonnade.

Rosa filipes 'Kiftsgate'
◐ ❊ ❖ SUMMER-FLOWERING, AUTUMN HIPS
H 15m (49ft) S 8m (26ft)

This is a real giant of a rose, with long, thorny stems and pointed, mid-green leaves, yet it has a daintiness – especially in the airiness of its large sprays of flowers. The semi-double, creamy-white, fragrant blooms are carried in open sprays that can be 80cm (32in) long and 60cm (2ft) wide. Small, orange-red hips sometimes follow. Too vigorous for small gardens, this sturdy, disease-resistant Rambler is at its best growing into large trees and over unsightly buildings.

'Francis E. Lester'
❊ ❖ SUMMER-FLOWERING, AUTUMN HIPS
H 5m (16ft) S 3m (10ft)

This is a strong-growing Rambler with healthy, mid-green foliage. The small, single flowers are white, tinged shell pink at the edges, and carried in large, loose, strongly fragrant sprays. Small orange hips follow. A good choice for growing over a large shed or as a colonnade, it can also be grown as a shrub or hedge.

Roses for specific situations

Roses can be used in so many ways in the garden, not only in formal beds or mixed borders. Some make excellent decorative hedges and thorny barriers, others can be used as ground cover on banks and rough areas of ground in full sun, while many are excellent subjects for pots. We tend to think of roses as delicate beauties to be cosseted – and certainly there are some that have very specific likes and dislikes – but there are also plenty that are tough and versatile and that are bound to succeed in your garden, whatever the soil type and growing conditions.

Roses as ground cover

Roses with long, trailing stems that spread over the ground make ideal ground-cover plants. They're an excellent way of smothering uneven ground that's difficult to cultivate or contains building rubble, or covering up an old tree stump. They also look good growing on sunny banks and tumbling over low walls. Less rampant varieties can be used to add low mounds of colour at the front of large beds and borders and as cascading subjects for pots.

A good Ground-cover rose has plenty of stems that grow closely together and lots of healthy, disease-resistant foliage. The main reason to use a rose as ground cover is for its colourful flowers, so you want to select plants that flower freely and as continuously as possible all summer long, without the need for dead-heading.

The Flower Carpet roses are the most popular and successful varieties for ground cover. The original 'Flower Carpet Pink' has now been joined by a whole range of other colours, broadening the possibilities for their use in co-ordinated colour schemes. *Alchemilla mollis*, with dense mounds of foliage, makes a good planting companion for these roses, particularly the stronger-coloured varieties because its frothy green flowers soften and lighten their impact. Ground-cover geraniums, such as *Geranium* 'Jolly Bee' and 'Rozanne', also work well, their saucer-shaped blue flowers complementing any colour of rose. (For more ground-cover roses, *see* page 87).

Planting and maintenance

As with all successful ground-cover schemes, the secret of success is a weed-free site before you plant. If thorough ground preparation isn't possible, owing to the nature of the site, use a systemic non-residual herbicide to kill perennial weeds. Because of their thorny stems, weeding between Ground-cover roses is difficult, so it's a good idea to mulch around them after planting with a thick layer of bark chippings.

This works only on level sites. On slopes it's best to cover the ground with a weed-control membrane and plant through that. Most Ground-cover roses should be planted about 1m (40in) apart.

Ground-cover roses have to be able to thrive with little maintenance. Once established, access will be difficult during the growing season, without damage to the plants. You would have to walk over them to get to the heart of the plant to dead-head. Occasional pruning in winter or early spring to remove some of the older stems and encourage new growth should be all the maintenance they require. More compact varieties can be trimmed with a pair of shears to remove old flowerheads and encourage new flowering sideshoots. A generous application of rose fertilizer in spring, before growth gets going, helps to keep them in good shape.

'Grouse' is a healthy, vigorous Ground-cover rose with trailing stems, shiny green leaves and fragrant, single, pale pink flowers. It thrives on poor soil.

Roses for hedging

Many roses make excellent hedges, providing the colour, fragrance and informal habit lacking in most other hedging subjects. A rose hedge doesn't just act as a practical boundary around the edge of the garden. While it can form an impenetrable barrier that is excellent for security, it can also be a superb decorative feature, acting as a garden divider, lining a path, and adding a touch of formality to the overall picture.

'Wild Edric' may be a tough rose, but it produces a lovely display of flowers when grown as a hedge.

For a rose to make an attractive hedge it needs to have a bushy, well-branched habit and masses of disease-resistant foliage. Upright roses that have a tendency to be bare at the base don't form good hedges, nor do roses that need careful pruning to maintain their branch framework. Instead, you want tough, tolerant varieties that will respond to shears or a hedge trimmer. A good hedging rose should also be free-flowering, whether in one main flush in midsummer or in succession throughout the season.

Low, decorative hedges

A low rose hedge is a good way to divide different areas of the garden. The Gallica roses *Rosa gallica* var. *officinalis* and *Rosa gallica* 'Versicolor' are both compact, resilient plants that cope with difficult growing conditions. They flower only once in summer, but their foliage usually remains attractive and disease-free throughout the season. They're ideal alongside later-summer borders or shrubs and perennials that perform in the second half of the year. For a formal feel, try planting a second hedge of compact lavenders, such as *Lavandula angustifolia* 'Hidcote', alongside a line of Gallica roses.

Roses also look effective lining a path, or running along a narrow border. If you have a border 1m (3ft) or so wide, try planting a hedge of 'The Mayflower', which is easy to maintain and produces fragrant, double, pink blooms throughout summer.

Larger hedges

Taller, fuller hedges suit big, country gardens. Many larger-growing English roses are suitable for hedging, for instance 'Hyde Hall', which flowers freely throughout the season. The Hybrid Musk roses are also good, such as 'Cornelia', 'Penelope' and 'Felicia'. These are broad and spreading in habit, with sprays of deliciously fragrant flowers throughout summer. A hedge of any of these varieties would be a delight alongside a broad grass path.

Some species roses are well suited to planting as mixed hedges with other subjects, such as hawthorn (*Crataegus monogyna*), blackthorn (*Prunus spinosa*), spindle (*Euonymus europaeus*) and cornelian cherry (*Cornus mas*). The British native dog rose (*Rosa canina*) and the sweet briar (*Rosa rubiginosa*) are particularly suitable. This type of hedge suits rural situations and any naturalistic scheme. The roses add scented flowers in summer and hips in autumn; the sweet briar also has wonderful apple-scented foliage.

Good roses for hedges

LOW HEDGES (under 1m/3ft)
'De Rescht'
'Harlow Carr'
'Molineux'
'Queen of Sweden'
Rosa gallica var. *officinalis*
Rosa gallica 'Versicolor'
'Rosemoor'
'The Mayflower'

MEDIUM TO TALL HEDGES (over 1m/3ft)
'Bonica'
'Complicata'
'Cornelia'
'Iceberg'
'Wild Edric'
'Wisley 2008'

Boundary hedges

Roses with strong, thorny stems make excellent boundary hedges in both urban and rural areas. *Rosa rugosa* is frequently used for this purpose. It has upright stems with fine, pointed thorns, apple-green foliage and single or semi-double flowers in white, pink or purple-red. It also produces large, tomato-like hips that are still attractive after the leaves have fallen. For a broad, impenetrable barrier, plant them as a staggered double row, allowing 1m (3ft) between plants and 60cm (2ft) between the rows.

The larger cultivars, such as 'Roseraie de l'Haÿ' and 'Blanche Double de Coubert', also form excellent hedges but rarely produce good hips. Some English roses have *Rosa rugosa* in their parentage and make outstanding hedging plants, for example the semi-double, deep-pink 'Wild Edric'.

Hedge planting and aftercare

Roses planted as a hedge need the same careful attention as any other garden rose. Good soil preparation and the addition of plenty of well-rotted manure or garden compost provide the foundation for a hedge that will be a long-term garden feature. Roses have a broader spread than many other hedging plants, so they're generally grown as a single row of plants. Short varieties, which grow to less than 1m (3ft) high, should be planted about 50–70cm (20–28in) apart. Make sure you give more space to taller, more vigorous roses, planting them approximately 1–1.2m (3–4ft) apart.

A colourful screen of beautiful Shrub roses makes a lovely, soft boundary and offers so much more than a line of conifers, or broad-leaved evergreen hedging plants.

Because roses grown as a hedge are in close proximity to one another, feeding and watering in dry weather are particularly important if the roses are to repeat bloom during the season. As with all roses, prune hedges between late winter and early spring. The best approach when it comes to roses grown this way is to use sharp hedging shears or a hedge trimmer, cutting to 20–30cm (8–12in) below the desired height to allow for the current season's growth and flowers. Then tidy up with a pair of secateurs to remove any dead or damaged stems.

Rose hedges to attract wildlife

Many roses make good subjects to attract wildlife into your garden. Varieties with single and semi-double flowers are magnets for bees and pollinating insects, and those that produce hips are valuable sources of food for birds in winter. Large Shrub roses left to grow naturally provide safe havens for roosting and nesting birds.

Good roses for wildlife include the following:

'Complicata'
'Francis E. Lester'
Rosa moyesii
'Rambling Rector'

Rosa rubiginosa
Rosa rugosa (right)
'Wedding Day'
'Wild Edric'

Growing roses on garden structures

Climbing and Rambler roses lend themselves to training over structures and are a wonderful way of introducing a vertical dimension. They're particularly useful in small gardens, where ground space is limited. Arches, pergolas, arbours, obelisks, tripods, colonnades and pillars are all popular means of elevating roses to show off their attributes to maximum advantage. Roses can also be used to soften visually hard structures, such as walls, and disguise eyesores. For practical information on supporting roses, *see* pages 52–6.

'A Shropshire Lad' is just one of the many repeat-flowering English roses that can be grown as a climber up a pillar or around an arch or arbour.

Arches and pergolas

A rose arch or pergola is often considered a classic element of the English garden. When you're choosing such a structure, you first need to ensure it's robust enough to support the weight of a rose or roses in full growth. Some light, inexpensive garden kits are simply not strong enough to do the job. It also needs to be wide enough to allow easy passage through it when the sides are clothed with thorny rose stems. An arch that is 1m (40in) wide will have a passage only half that width in midsummer, which is barely sufficient if it is placed across a main pathway.

Next, you need to think carefully about where to position the garden structure. It needs to look 'intended'. For example, an arch looks natural where two boundaries meet, making it obvious that you're going from one part of the garden into the other, but it looks meaningless if positioned halfway along a path where there is no natural boundary. Think of it as part of the journey through the garden – a feature on the way to a destination. A pergola

The beautiful Rambler rose 'Adélaïde d'Orléans' turns a long pergola into a creamy-pink fairytale walkway – an unforgettable sight in midsummer.

Good roses for arches, arbours and pergolas

ARCH OR ARBOUR

'A Shropshire Lad'
'Graham Thomas'
'Phyllis Bide'
'Snow Goose'
'Teasing Georgia'

PERGOLA

'Adélaïde d'Orléans'
'Crimson Shower'
'Iceberg'
'Malvern Hills'
'Paul Noël'

could lead to a seat, a statue or a doorway, while an arch could be a gateway to another interesting part of the garden.

You also need to think about how the arch or pergola will be anchored into the planting. The secret of success with any structure is to pay as much attention to what you plant around it as to what you grow over it. An arch covered with roses with no planting at the base looks top-heavy, and underplanting balances it. Choose shade-loving plants, especially low-growing evergreens, because these enhance the planting picture in winter.

Arbours

A garden arbour, basically a seat within an arch, is usually positioned against a wall or fence or against a backdrop of other planting. This is a place to sit and enjoy the garden, so scent is an important quality to consider. You could combine a fragrant rose with honeysuckle, jasmine and lilies. Avoid extremely thorny kinds and really vigorous varieties that require lots of maintenance. The lovely, soft-gold 'Goldfinch' would be a good choice, as would the bluish-mauve, scented 'Veilchenblau'. Both of these are summer-flowering. For continuous blooms, look to the English Roses that can be grown as climbers (see pages 18 and 102–5).

Colonnades

If you haven't got space for an arch or pergola, you can create a similar effect along a boundary, at the back of a border or between garden areas with a colonnade. This is a series of

The deliciously fragrant 'Rambling Rector' makes a magnificent feature trained on rope swags to create a colonnade effect.

posts linked by swagged ropes, which the roses are tied to as they grow, resulting in elevated garlands of roses. (See also page 55.) Colonnades suit formal gardens, but also fit surprisingly well into more rustic settings if you use subtle, round posts and natural ropes. As with any scheme using Climbing or Rambler roses, the flowering season can be extended with the addition of clematis (see pages 42–3). Vigorous *Clematis viticella* hybrids work well here, such as the soft-purple *Clematis* 'Purpurea Plena Elegans'.

Good roses for colonnades

'Albéric Barbier'
'Félicité Perpétué'
'Francis E. Lester'
'Rambling Rector'
'The Garland'
'Wedding Day'

Pillars, obelisks and rustic tripods

Roses that are grown as pillars or up decorative obelisks are a good way to add height to a planting scheme and to showcase the blooms of the rose. They work well in narrow borders, alongside paths and rising out of beds with low plantings of short-growing roses and perennials. You need to choose short Climbing roses with upright stems that can be controlled, otherwise the feature will be swamped and the effect will be lost (see page 116).

Rustic tripods suit large, informal gardens, and make useful freestanding structures in rough grass. They are a good way to grow bushy Climbing or Rambler roses and large, arching Shrub roses. A heavy tripod of rustic poles provides just enough support for the strong but somewhat unruly stems of the

The English rose 'The Pilgrim' has a long
flowering period and is an excellent
choice for a pillar in sun or shade.

rose, and the blooms are carried
along the stems that loosely arch
out from the tripod supports. Roses
that are grown in this way need less
maintenance by way of tying in and
training than those climbing up
pillars and obelisks or over arches.

Doorways

Many of us dream of our front
doorway surrounded by a beautiful
fragrant rose. In reality, this is often
a struggling specimen supported by
a piece of unattractive trellis. If
you're going to be successful with
roses in this situation, you need a
sensible planting space at least

'New Dawn' has flexible stems that
are easy to train over a doorway,
where the pretty pale pink flowers
are displayed beautifully.

80cm (32in) square, with good soil,
alongside the front door, and you'll
need to wire the wall for support
(*see* page 56).

If you're going to train a rose
around a doorway, choose a variety
suitable for a rose arch (*see* page
114). Avoid an upright variety;
instead, choose one with flexible,
arching stems. 'New Dawn' is always
a good bet for its healthy dark green
foliage and continuous pink flowers.
Yellow roses attract attention, so are
good at emphasizing doorways:
'The Pilgrim' flowers freely, is
disease-resistant, and also succeeds
in shade. If the door is painted,
you'll always create more impact by
either coordinating or contrasting
the colour of the door with that
of the rose.

Don't forget

If you don't have space to grow a Climbing
rose in the ground by a doorway you could
grow a modest-growing climber in a large
pot (see page 119).

Good roses for pillars,
obelisks and tripods

PILLAR OR OBELISK

'A Shropshire Lad'
'Crown Princess Margareta'
'Gertrude Jekyll'
'Madame Isaac Pereire'
'The Pilgrim'
'Warm Welcome'

RUSTIC TRIPOD

'Albertine'
'Complicata'
'Geranium'
'New Dawn'
'Snow Goose'
'William Lobb'

Walls

Most Climbing and Rambler roses will thrive and bloom profusely against a sunny, south- or west-facing wall. North- and east-facing walls need a little more thought; if they get only a few hours sun in summer, choose a rose suitable for a shady wall (*see* page 120).

It's also important to select a rose of the right vigour and habit for the wall. Some Climbing roses have a very upright habit and are therefore best for high walls. 'Madame Alfred Carrière', for example, has strong, upright stems that resent horizontal training. It's a fantastic choice for a high wall or the gable-end of a house, but wouldn't work on a low wall or fence, or trained over an arch. The Rambler rose 'Phyllis Bide', on the other hand, has flexible stems that are amenable to horizontal training. It could easily be trained along wires that are fixed to a fence

Seen at its best cllimbing up a high, sunny wall, 'Lady Hillingdon' is a wonderfully fragrant Tea rose.

or wall lower than 1.5m (5ft). Most of the English roses that can be grown as climbers can also be used in this way.

Covering eyesores

Strong-growing Rambler roses are at home scrambling over buildings, and can be used to conceal eyesores such as garages, large sheds and outbuildings. As their blooms are never lovelier than when looked down on from above, this is a wonderful way to enjoy them.

When planting a rose to cover a building, you need to remember that the rose will be a heavy weight to bear once in full growth, and that the structure needs to be sufficiently strong to stand that load. The average timber garden shed is not resilient enough to support the

weight of a strong-growing Rambler. If it is a structure like this that you're trying to enhance, choose a small, light Rambler rose, such as 'Malvern Hills' or 'Snow Goose', rather than one of the more vigorous varieties recommended (*see* page 118). Also, bear in mind other practicalities such as access to and maintenance of the structure. For instance, a very vigorous Rambler, such as 'Bobbie James', is not a good choice to scramble over your oil tank, as you'll have immense difficulty getting to it. When planting a rose to scramble over a building, plant and support the rose as you would against a wall (*see* page 56). When the stems reach

Good roses for walls

LOW WALLS (under 2m/6ft)
'Golden Gate'
'Goldfinch'
'New Dawn'
'Phyllis Bide'
'Snow Goose'
'The Prince's Trust'
'Warm Welcome'

HIGH WALLS (2–4m/6–12ft)
'Albéric Barbier'
'Albertine'
'Cécile Brünner'
'Compassion'
'Crimson Glory'
'Étoile de Hollande'
'Lady Hillingdon'
'Madame Alfred Carrière'

'Wedding Day' smothers a building in a fragrant blanket of creamy flowers followed by orange-red hips.

as 'Albéric Barbier', are almost evergreen and screen more effectively in winter. Others, like 'Wedding Day' and 'Rambling Rector', produce attractive hips that add interest in autumn and winter.

Growing roses through trees

Strong-growing Rambler roses naturally scramble through the branches of a tree and have a wild beauty when grown in this way. A strong, mature tree can be given another dimension and season of interest with the blooms of a rose to enhance its foliage. The first consideration is to match the vigour of the rose to the tree. Large, mature trees, such as sycamore (*Acer pseudoplatanus*) and ash (*Fraxinus*), make good supports for really rampant Climbing roses, while smaller trees, like flowering crabs and old apple trees (*Malus*), can support some of the less vigorous Ramblers. These can also be grown over the branches of dead trees, turning them into attractive features.

It's also important to think about the effect of rose flowers against a tree's foliage. Trees with large, plain green leaves, such as the common sycamore, look best adorned with small, white flowers; the rose blooms lighten the foliage and the tree's leaves display the flowers to best advantage. Purple-leaved trees, such as some crab apples and ornamental cherries (*Prunus*), as well as red-leaved Norway maples (*Acer platanoides*), are particularly effective combined with red- or pink-flowered Ramblers, such as 'American Pillar' or 'Crimson Shower'.

The cerise-pink flowers of 'American Pillar' light up the branches of a purple-leaved *Malus* in midsummer.

For information on planting and supporting roses against a tree, *see* pages 50 and 54. For pruning information, *see* page 63, although in most cases roses in trees are generally left to their own devices.

the roof, or the top of the structure, they will throw themselves over it and cling on.

Most roses don't look their best in winter, and as they lose their leaves they won't provide an effective screen for an eyesore, particularly in the first couple of years. Some, such

Good roses for garages, large sheds or outbuildings

'Albéric Barbier'
'Francis E. Lester'
'Malvern Hills'
'Rambling Rector'
'Wedding Day'

Don't forget

A rose growing over a roof or a building will hold on to moisture beneath its stems and leaves, especially if fallen leaves and petals are left to collect on the surface and they start to decay. This can cause problems, particularly on timber sheds with felt roofs.

Good roses for trees

FOR LARGE TREES
Rosa banksiae 'Lutea'
'Bobbie James'
Rosa filipes 'Kiftsgate'
'Paul's Himalayan Musk'
'Rambling Rector'

FOR SMALLER TREES
'American Pillar'
'Crimson Shower'
'Kew Rambler'
'Paul Noël'
'Wedding Day'

Roses in containers

Even if you don't have any space for roses in the open ground, you can enjoy them in pots on the patio, doorstep or balcony. Alternatively, try growing a few roses in containers close to a seating area, where you can enjoy their exquisite and often fragrant flowers at close hand. Roses are more rewarding in pots than many seasonal bedding plants, and with a little care should bloom throughout the summer months, year after year.

Choosing roses and containers

Any Patio roses and compact Floribundas are good choices for pots, as are some of the smaller English roses. These are usually more fragrant and have a more graceful habit. When choosing a rose for a container, look for a specimen that has a compact, bushy habit, repeat flowers well and has healthy foliage; this is always more visible when you show off an individual plant in a container. Containers for most roses should be at least 40cm (16in) wide and deep, and able to hold about 25 litres of compost.

Miniature roses are useful for very small spaces and are sometimes raised as house plants. Some are charming, compact shrubs that bloom almost continuously from early summer through to autumn.

A Climbing rose in a pot is a good way to introduce colour and fragrance against the wall of the house, perhaps alongside a doorway. Often there is no soil here to allow you to plant directly into the open ground, so a container is the only solution. Select a relatively compact rose that will not get too big (*see* box, left), and choose a very large pot, because a Climbing rose can make a lot of growth.

Planting and aftercare

When planting a rose in a pot, use a loam-based compost such as John Innes No. 3. Plant to the same depth as you would roses in the ground (*see* page 48). Add a handful of rose food to the compost at planting, and repeat in midsummer. Water new roses well before and after planting, and regularly from spring to mid-autumn. Each spring, scrape away the top 5cm (2in) of compost and replenish with fresh John Innes and rose fertilizer. Prune as you would roses in the ground.

The red Ground-cover rose 'Suffolk' makes a colourful, showy subject for a hanging basket.

Good roses for pots

MODERN BUSH AND SHRUB ROSES

'Amber Queen'
'Ballerina'
'Darcey Bussell'
'Flower Carpet Pink'
'Grace'
'Margaret Merril'
'Queen Mother '
'Sweet Dream'
'Young Lycidas'

MINIATURE ROSES

'Lavender Jewel'
'Little Flirt'
'Mr Bluebird'
'Pour Toi'
'Stars 'n' Stripes'

CLIMBING AND RAMBLER ROSES

'Golden Gate'
'Snow Goose'
'Teasing Georgia'
'The Prince's Trust'
'Warm Welcome'

Don't forget

Roses don't like to be crowded, so avoid mixing them with other plants, even seasonal bedding, in a container. To create exciting combinations, group pots together.

Large tubs of cerise-pink roses bring fragrance and a welcome splash of colour to the patio in summer.

Roses for challenging sites

All gardeners would love to have a sunny, sheltered garden with that deep, well-drained, fertile soil that you read about in books. In reality, few have ideal conditions, but that won't stop you wanting to grow roses. The ancestors of the garden rose have been around for millions of years, having survived major climatic changes and adverse conditions in the wild, so roses are generally adaptable creatures. If you have a shady or exposed site, or a particularly dry or wet soil, it's just a matter of selecting tough varieties that will cope with such situations.

The Climbing rose 'Madame Alfred Carrière' produces its lovely, fragrant, ivory blooms even in shady situations, although it won't tolerate dense shade.

Growing roses in shade

Most roses thrive in a situation that enjoys at least four hours of direct sunshine a day from mid-spring through to mid-autumn; the Modern Bush roses in particular prefer lots of sunshine. However, many roses will grow and bloom quite satisfactorily with less than four hours direct sun, providing that the site isn't overshadowed by the branches of mature trees or the overhang of a building. Most repeat-flowering Shrub roses fall into this category, particularly the English roses, Rugosa roses and Hybrid Musk roses, such as 'Felicia' and 'Buff Beauty'. Where direct sunlight is minimal, rose growth will be lighter and may be rather drawn; flowers will be fewer but they will still be produced. The secret of success is to compensate by giving your roses more space around the plants and making sure that they don't go short of fertilizer and water during the growing season.

Roses with other plants in shade

It's a good idea to combine roses with other plants in shade, to compensate for the fact that there are often fewer flowers and to provide interest once the rose has finished flowering. Light, bright roses, particularly yellow ones, are a good choice for shade because they show up well in low light and help to brighten up a dark corner. 'The Pilgrim', which can be grown as a shrub or as a short climber, is an excellent choice for shade. Trained up a pillar, it makes a striking focal point against a background of dark evergreen foliage, such as yew (*Taxus*). It also looks good against a wall, alongside a large-leaved ivy, such as *Hedera colchica* 'Sulphur Heart', which has dark green foliage boldly splashed with emerald and gold. In winter the ivy adds colour, and in summer it provides an attractive backdrop for the flowers.

Similarly, the clear golden-yellow *Rosa* 'Molineux' looks striking combined with the gold-and-green variegated dogwood *Cornus sericea* 'Hedgerows Gold'. Underplant it with *Euonymus fortunei* 'Emerald 'n' Gold' or *Vinca minor* 'Illumination' and you accentuate the effect in summer and maintain it during winter, when the rose and dogwood leaves have fallen.

Foxgloves (*Digitalis*) grow well in situations lightly shaded by trees and associate well with roses that tolerate some shade. The purple-pink *Digitalis purpurea* looks glorious with the grey-green leaves and semi-double pink flowers of *Rosa* 'Königin von Dänemark', and the strawberry-pink, double, scented *Rosa* 'Cornelia' is delightful with the apricot-pink *Digitalis purpurea* 'Sutton's Apricot'.

Roses on poor, dry soils

Sandy soils and shallow, chalky soils both tend to be dry and low in nutrients; not ideal conditions for growing roses. In both cases, they can be improved by the addition of plenty of well-rotted manure dug in before planting and then applied as a mulch on a regular basis (*see* pages 46–7); this will improve the texture and also lower the soil pH, which is good for roses as they prefer a slightly acid soil. Regular feeding is also essential, as nutrients are washed easily from the soil.

However well you nourish your soil, there is no doubt that some roses are better adapted to these conditions than others, and it's always better to choose these rather than opting for the fussy, high-maintenance varieties. 'Madame Knorr' ('Comte de Chambord') is a

tough little repeat-flowering Shrub rose ideal for the smaller garden. It's very disease-resistant and reliable in sun or partial shade. *Berberis thunbergii* f. *atropurpurea* 'Rose Glow', with its red-purple leaves, would make an excellent planting partner for it on a dry, sandy or alkaline soil. *Rosa* 'Marchesa Boccella' ('Jacques Cartier') is similar but with fewer, larger flowers; it is just as tough and reliable.

Alternatively, you could choose the English rose 'The Mayflower'. This has *Rosa rugosa* in its parentage, making it very suitable for sandy or chalky soils. The tough English roses

suitable for hedging, such as 'Rosemoor' and 'Wild Edric', also succeed on poor, dry soils.

Thought of more as a foliage shrub than a rose in the traditional sense, the species rose *Rosa glauca* is very useful on poor, dry soils. Its arching dark stems and striking, steely blue-green foliage are its main attribute, but its single, dark cerise-pink flowers and reddish autumn hips are not without charm. It contrasts well with any purple foliage shrubs and is lovely with silver. Try it with the catmint *Nepeta* 'Six Hills Giant' and the bright cerise *Geranium psilostemon*.

Roses for poor, dry soils

SHRUB ROSES
'Buff Beauty'
'Fru Dagmar Hastrup'
Rosa glauca
'Madame Knorr'
'Marchesa Boccella'
Rosa × *odorata* 'Mutabilis'
'Rosemoor'
'The Mayflower'
'Wild Edric'

CLIMBING AND RAMBLER ROSES
Rosa banksiae 'Lutea'
'Lady Hillingdon'
'Madame Alfred Carrière'
'Phyllis Bide'

Rosa glauca may not have the showiest of blooms, but it has striking blue-green leaves and thrives on poor, dry soils. Here it makes a wonderful planting partner for foxgloves and geraniums.

Roses in exposed situations

There's one advantage to growing roses in exposed, windy situations: they're less likely to suffer from diseases such as mildew and black spot, because there's plenty of air circulation around the plants. However, roses can suffer in exposed situations, mainly because they lack a dense, fibrous root system, so if a plant rocks in the wind it can become unstable – the long, woody roots will become dislodged, and fragile sideshoots can break off, which can be detrimental. Wind can also damage the flowers, particularly larger varieties with soft petals.

If you garden on a windy site, it's best to choose strong-growing, stocky plants with smaller, short-petalled flowers. The compact-growing, repeat-flowering Shrub rose 'Fru Dagmar Hastrup', which has single, pink flowers and large, orange-red hips, succeeds on exposed sites. The bushy, pink,

double English rose 'Harlow Carr' is also excellent. It forms a rounded shrub up to 1.2m (4ft) high, with flowers continuously produced all over the shrub. Both would work well planted against a backdrop of the evergreen shrub *Elaeagnus × ebbingei*, whose waxy grey-green leaves are extremely wind- and weather-resistant.

It's well worth staking taller Floribundas and Shrub roses with stout, wooden posts to prevent wind rock in more exposed situations (*see* page 52). It also pays to tidy the plants in autumn to remove any heavy top-growth, which will put up resistance to the wind and rock the plants. Just cut back by around 20 per cent, removing any fading flowers and buds and shortening long, twiggy stems.

Since Climbing and Rambler roses are often protected by their supports, they're not as much of a problem in exposed sites as bushy, freestanding roses.

Coastal gardens

Gardens by the coast generally produce excellent roses, often earlier than gardens inland because the weather tends to be a degree or two warmer. Also, light levels are often high because of the lack of tree cover. If soil is fertile, and the garden is sheltered, there is no need to worry about selecting particular varieties. However, if the soil is sandy, and the situation windy, it's best to opt for varieties of *Rosa rugosa*. The species is a native of sea shores in Japan, so it's well prepared to deal with this situation.

The Scots rose, *Rosa spinosissima* (previously *Rosa pimpinellifolia*) is a British native of cliffs near to the sea. It forms mounds of small, dark leaves studded with small, white flowers in late spring. There are various cultivars with flowers in shades of pink and pale yellow. Most grow to around 1–1.5m (3–5ft) high and are ideal for the most exposed coastal gardens. 'Stanwell Perpetual' is

Roses for exposed situations

'Ballerina'
'Bonica'
'Charles de Mills'
'Fru Dagmar Hastrup'
Rosa gallica var. *officinalis*
'Harlow Carr'
'Port Sunlight'
'Queen of Sweden'
'The Mayflower'

The English rose 'Harlow Carr' blooms freely and continuously in exposed situations where other roses fail.

particularly worth seeking out for its blush-pink flowers that are produced throughout the summer.

Roses for cold, wet conditions

Few garden plants grow well on heavy, waterlogged soils and roses are no exception. Providing there's reasonable drainage, some hardy roses cope well with cold, wet conditions and these are the ones to choose if the climate in your area is that way inclined.

Where summers are more often cool and wet rather than warm and sunny, it's best to avoid roses with very double flowers and thin petals. These are prone to balling (*see* page 75) and in a bad year you may well never see a rose bloom that opens

The glorious Rambler rose 'Félicité Perpétué', with its cream to pale pink flowers on red stems, is a tolerant subject that copes with both dry and heavy, wet soils. Whatever the growing conditions, it flowers freely and remains free of disease.

Don't forget

If in doubt, play safe and choose a tough, reliable rose. Varieties of *Rosa × alba*, *Rosa gallica* and *Rosa rugosa* seem to succeed in just about any situation, however poor the soil or hostile the growing conditions.

Roses for cold, wet conditions

SHRUB ROSES
Rosa × alba 'Alba Semiplena'
'De Rescht'
'Maiden's Blush'
'Marchesa Boccella'
Rosa rugosa 'Alba'
'Wild Edric'

CLIMBING AND RAMBLER ROSES
'Albéric Barbier'
'Bobbie James'
'Cécile Brünner'
'Félicité Perpétué'
'Madame Alfred Carrière'

properly. Instead, opt for roses with semi-double flowers that open fully and quickly from the bud stage.

The Alba roses, with upright growth and tough, blue-green foliage, are particularly good in cold, wet conditions and remain free of disease. The lovely *Rosa × alba* 'Alba Semiplena', with pure white, semi-double, fragrant flowers is very

weather-resistant and shows up well in low light. 'Maiden's Blush', with soft-pink, fragrant flowers and the same blue-green foliage, is another excellent choice.

Also, any of the adaptable Rugosa roses are a good bet in cold, wet gardens. Their tough foliage seems to be very disease-resistant in all weather conditions.

Index

Page numbers in *italics* refer to plants described in the A–Z directory of recommended roses.

pruning saw 57
Prunus × *cistena* 31–2
Pulmonaria 28
purple spotting 75

R

rabbits 71
Rambler roses 12, 22, 23
  cold, wet conditions 123
  cultivars 106–9
  growing conditions 46
  growing through trees 50, 54, 118
  growth habits 13, 22
  planting 50
  poor, dry soils 121
  pruning and training 22, 30, 62–3,
    77, 117
  shady situations 120
  see also Climbing roses
red spider mite 73
Redouté, Pierre-Joseph 9–10
repeat-flowering roses 14, 15, 79,
  83–7
replant sickness 50, 70, 74
Rhodochiton atrosanguineus 43
RHS Rosemoor, Devon 11
rootstocks 58, 68
Rosa
  'A Shropshire Lad' 18, 30, *102*, 114,
    116
  'A Whiter Shade of Pale' *93*
  'Absolutely Fabulous' 35, *97*
  'Adélaïde d'Orléans' *106*, 114
  'Alan Titchmarsh' *88*
  × *alba* 'Alba Semiplena' 16, 27, 38,
    79, *80*, 123
  'Albéric Barbier' 36, 65, 67, *106*,
    115, 117, 118, 120, 123
  'Albertine' 30, 67, *106*, 116, 117
  'Alec's Red' 19, 25, *93*
  'Alexandre Girault' *106*
  'Alister Stella Gray' *102*
  'Altissimo' *102*
  'Amber Queen' *97*, 119
  'American Pillar' *106*, 118
  'Arthur Bell' 20, *97*
  'Ballerina' 40, 64, 65, *83*, 119, 122
  banksiae 'Lutea' *107*, 118, 121
  'Belle de Crécy' *80*
  'Blanche Double de Coubert' *83*, 113
  'Blue for You' *97*
  'Bobbie James' 23, *107*, 117, 118,
    123

'Bonica' 40, 43, *83*, 112, 122
'Brave Heart' 27, 65, *97*
'Bright Smile' *101*
'Buff Beauty' 36, 40, *83*, 120, 121
canina 16, 112
'Cardinal de Richelieu' *80*
'Cécile Brünner' 50, *102*, 117,
  123
'Celsiana' 16, *80*
× *centifolia* 'Cristata' 15, 17, *80*
'Champagne Moments' *98*
'Charles de Mills' 14, *81*, 122
'Charlotte' *88*
chinensis 'Mutabilis' *see Rosa* ×
  odorata 'Mutabilis'
'Claire Austin' 35, *88*
'Compassion' *102*, 117
'Complicata' 30, 67, *81*, 112, 113,
  116
'Comte de Chambord' *see* 'Madame
  Knorr'
'Cornelia' *84*, 112, 120, 121
'Crimson Glory' *103*, 117
'Crimson Shower' *107*, 114, 118
'Crocus Rose' *88*
'Crown Princess Margareta' 27, 30,
  89, 116
damascena 16
'Darcey Bussell' 27, 65, *89*, 119
'De Rescht' *84*, 112, 120, 123
'Elina' 25, *93*
'Elizabeth Harkness' 25, 79, *93*
'Escapade' *98*
'Étoile de Hollande' 22, 79, *103*,
  117
'Evelyn Fison' 33, 39, *98*
'Felicia' 16, 36, 40, *84*, 112, 120
'Félicité Perpétué' 23, 65, *107*, 115,
  120, 123
'Ferdinand Pichard' 15, 16, *84*
filipes 'Kiftsgate' *107*, 118
'Flower Carpet Pink' 65, *87*, 119
'Flower Carpet White' 39, 65, *87*
'Fragrant Cloud' 10
'Fragrant Delight' *98*
'Francis E. Lester' 12, *107*, 113, 115,
  118
'François Juranville' 67
'Freedom' *94*
'Fru Dagmar Hastrup' 41, *84*, 113,
  121, 122
gallica var. *officinalis* 9, 16, *81*, 112,
  122

gallica 'Versicolor' 9, 16, *82*, 112
'Gentle Hermione' *89*
'Geranium' *81*, 116
'Gertrude Jekyll' 18, 25, 42, 69, 79,
  89, 116
'Ghislane de Féligonde' *108*
glauca 41, 121
'Gloire de Dijon' 17
'Golden Celebration' 18, 25, 40, 65,
  79, *89*, 120
'Golden Gate' 43, *103*, 117, 119
'Golden Showers' *103*, 120
'Golden Wedding' *98*
'Golden Wings' 41, *84*
'Goldfinch' *108*, 115, 117
'Grace' *89*, 119
'Graham Thomas' 18, 25, 27, 31,
  65, *90*, 114
'Grandpa Dickson' *94*
'Greenall's Glory' 65, *101*
'Grouse 2000' *87*, 111
'Harlow Carr' 38, 41, *90*, 112, 122
'Help for Heroes' 39, *98*
'Heritage' 18
'Hyde Hall' 112
'Iceberg' 20, 21, 34, 65, *99*, *103*,
  112, 114
'Impératrice Joséphine' *81*
'Ipsilante' *82*
'Jacqueline du Pré' *85*
'Jacques Cartier' *see* 'Marchesa
  Boccella'
'James Galway' *103*
'Jubilee Celebration' 18, 39, 60, *90*
'Julia's Rose' 19, *94*
'Just Joey' 25, *94*
'Kew Rambler' *108*, 118
'King's Macc' *94*
'Königin von Dänemark' 27, 34, *82*,
  120
'Korresia' *99*
'La France' 10
'L'Aimant' *99*
'Lady Emma Hamilton' 27, 33, *90*
'Lady Hillingdon' 42, *104*, 117, 121
'Lady of Shalott' *90*
'Lavender Jewel' 119
'Lilli Marlene' 10
'Little Flirt' 119
'Lucky' *99*
'Madame Alfred Carrière' 22, 56,
  104, 117, 120, 121, 123
'Madame Hardy' *82*

Acknowledgements

BBC Books and OutHouse would like to thank the following for their assistance in preparing this book: Phil McCann for advice and guidance; Robin Whitecross for picture research; Candida Frith-Macdonald for help with illustrations; Lesley Riley for proofreading; Marie Lorimer for the index.

Picture credits

Key t = top, b = bottom, l = left, r = right, c = centre

PHOTOGRAPHS

All photographs by Jonathan Buckley (including page 27 in conjunction with National Trust Picture Library) except those listed below.

David Austin Roses 4, 5, 8, 9, 11t, 12, 13, 15t, 16a, b, d, e, f & g, 17a, c, d, e & g, 18, 19t, 22, 23, 33cl, tr & br, 34tl & bl, 38b, 42cl, bl & tr, 43tr & br, 60, 65, 69t, 79, 80, 81, 82, 83, 84, 85tl, tc, bl, c & r, 86, 87tl, tc, bl, c & r, 88, 89, 90, 91, 92, 93, 94, 95tl, c & r, bl & br, 96tl & tr, bl, c & r, 97tc, tr & br, 98tl, c, r & bl, 99tl, c, r, bl & br, 100tc, tr, bl & br, 101, 102, 103, 104, 105tl, tc, bl, c & r, 106l, tc, bc & br, 107, 108, 109, 111, 112, 114, 116t, 117, 122, 123

Bridgeman Art Library 10t

GAP Photos Richard Bloom 35tr, 97l; Mark Bolton 29, 106tr; Elke Borkowski 33cr, 43tl; Lynne Brotchie 24(2), 25t; Nicola Browne 17f; Sarah Cuttle 100tl; Paul Debois 20tl, 97bc; John Glover 19b, 67, 87tr, 115, 119t; Anne Green-Armytage 113t; Jerry Harpur 10b, 20b, 28, 39, 40, 119b; Marcus Harpur 121; Martin Hughes-Jones 17b, 33tl; Janet Johnson 113b; Lynn Keddie 32; Geoff Kidd 20tr; Jenny Lilly 35cl, 99bc; Zara Napier 16c & h, 17i, 34cr, 118l; Jonathan Need 96tc; Clive Nichols 26, 42br, 43bl; Howard Rice 17h, 98bc, 100bc, 105tr, 116b, 120; Sabina Ruber 85tr; JS Sira 11b, 34br, 42cr; S&O 36, 37b; Dave Zubraski 64, 95bc

Andrew Lawson 110

Marianne Majerus Garden Images Marianne Majerus 2–3, 14, 38t

Andrew McIndoe 33bl, 34cl, 35tl & cr, 37t, 98br, 118r

Nature Photographers Ltd Richard Revels 70

Anthony Tesselaar Plants 15b

Robin Whitecross 45

ILLUSTRATIONS

Lizzie Harper 57, 58, 60, 61, 63, 72tl, ct, cb, tr, rc & br, 73, 74, 75

Susan Hillier 72lb, 75br

Janet Tanner 12, 13, 30, 45, 48t & b, 49, 50, 52, 53, 54, 55, 56, 57, 59, 60, 66, 67

Thanks are also due to the following designers and owners, whose gardens appear in the book:

Bankton Cottage, Sussex 14; Castle Howard 26; Bob Clark 10b; Coughton Court 2–3; Helen Dillon 39; Danae Duthy, Country Roses, Essex 24l, 25b, 69b; Hemingford Grey Manor, Cambridgeshire 38t; Keith Kirsten 119b; Rani Lall, Oxford 35b; Christopher Lloyd, Great Dixter, East Sussex 41; Joy Martin 120; The National Trust, Sissinghurst Castle Gardens, Kent 27; Dan Pearson 17f; Elaine and David Rolfe, Ochran Mill, Gwent 21; Nick Ryan, London SW12 50; Sue and Wol Staines, Glen Chantry, Essex 31